The IEA Health and We

Choice in Welfare No. 27

Community Without Politics

A Market Approach to Welfare Reform

David G. Green

IEA Health and Welfare Unit
London, 1996

First published January 1996

The IEA Health and Welfare Unit
2 Lord North St
London SW1P 3LB

ISBN 0-255 36364-8

Typeset by the IEA Health and Welfare Unit
in Palatino 11 point
Printed in Great Britain by
St Edmundsbury Press Ltd
Blenheim Industrial Park, Newmarket Rd
Bury St Edmunds, Suffolk

Contents

The Author

Dr David Green is the Director of the Health and Welfare Unit at the Institute of Economic Affairs. He was formerly a Labour councillor in Newcastle upon Tyne from 1976 until 1981, and from 1981 to 1983 was a Research Fellow at the Australian National University in Canberra.

His books include *Power and Party in an English City*, Allen & Unwin, 1980; *Mutual Aid or Welfare State*, Allen & Unwin, 1984, with L. Cromwell; *Working Class Patients and the Medical Establishment*, Temple Smith/Gower, 1985; and *The New Right: The Counter Revolution in Political, Economic and Social Thought*, Wheatsheaf, 1987. His work has also been published in journals such as *The Journal of Social Policy, Political Quarterly, Philosophy of the Social Sciences* and *Policy and Politics*.

The IEA has published his *The Welfare State: For Rich or for Poor*, 1982; *Which Doctor?*, 1985; *Challenge to the NHS*, 1986; *Medicines in the Marketplace*, 1987; *Everyone a Private Patient*, 1988; *Should Doctors Advertise?*, 1989; *Equalizing People*, 1990; *Medicard: A Better Way to Pay for Medicines?*, 1993 (with David Lucas); and *Reinventing Civil Society*, 1993.

Acknowledgements

I have benefited greatly from comments made by several colleagues, including Ralph Harris, Arthur Seldon, Professor Harold Rose, John Blundell, Colin Robinson, Robert Whelan, Lisa MacLellan, Nicky Tynan, Professor Peter Saunders, Professor David Conway, Tom Griffin, Sir Reginald Murley and Max Hartwell.

This book is based on a report originally produced for the New Zealand Business Roundtable, and my greatest debt is to its Executive Director, Roger Kerr, from whom I have learnt a great deal.

David G. Green

Preface

DESPITE the collapse of communism and near-universal support for a market economy over a planned economy, we are still at a crossroads between a free society and a collectivised order, chiefly because the state plays such a dominating role in health, education and welfare.

The main purpose of this book is to examine whether there is a viable private, non-political alternative to the welfare state. To that end, it describes the ideal of private welfare which, before the advent of the welfare state, permitted the government an essential but limited role whilst the chief burden was assumed by the unpoliticised community. Inevitably, to suggest the possibility of a reduced role for government in welfare will provoke opponents to resort to the usual array of caricatures of 'the market'. Consequently, the book also describes what I take to be the true liberal ethos and differentiates it from some modern doctrines which seem initially to resemble it.

A market economy on its own is not enough. This is not to imply that a competitive market lacks moral legitimacy. Far from it, a system of voluntary exchange is based on respect for the preferences of other people; and a market economy by comparison with a planned economy, helps to disperse productive resources, thus reducing the potential for the abuse of concentrated power and increasing opportunities for human creativity. Of equal importance, wide property ownership means that people are not beholden to government, so that 'public opinion' means a genuinely independent sphere of thought which can develop without fear or favour.

These are powerful arguments in its favour, quite apart from the happy coincidence that a market economy increases prosperity. But to put the matter at its simplest, a society which allows some people to become very wealthy must also place strong moral obligations on those who—whether through luck or judgement—are successful. They should be willing to come to the aid of the less fortunate. That is, the moral legitimacy of a free society rests not only on the attractions of liberty but also on acceptance of duty.

Quite apart from the conviction that duties should attend success, the twentieth century has also taught us that, if welfare assistance is provided primarily by the state, it often makes matters worse. But we are not left with a stark choice between 'state' and 'individual' responsibility. Before the welfare state there was an older ethos of 'community without politics' which, until the twentieth century, was an indispensable element of classical liberalism. In short, champions of liberty divided responsibility three ways: there was, first, individual or family responsibility; second, the community as distinct from the state; and third, the government. The majority of the population assumed responsibility for fostering a 'public but not political domain' of duties to care for all those who were not able to support themselves for one reason or another.

The establishment of the welfare state is often presented as a socialist success story as step-by-step the taxes for new services were dragged from a reluctant capitalist system. This theory holds true as an account of the ambition of socialists, but it exaggerates the reluctance of capitalists. Many of the rich wanted an expanded welfare state because they shared Bismarck's calculation that 'social reform' was necessary to buy off the potentially rebellious workers. This tradition of Tory paternalism was quite at home with class-war collectivism because both traditions shared a fundamental assumption: that the masses needed to have their lives managed for them by the authorities. They differed only about *who* should lead: for the Tory paternalists those of the best breeding or demonstrated ability should lead; for Labour, the workers or their representatives should be in charge.

Such were the dominant assumptions of the 'age of collectivism' which followed the collapse of liberalism early this century. But the political tradition on which Britain's prosperity and respect in the world was built was very different. For hundreds of years the dominant political ethos in Britain had understood the purpose of government to be, not management of people's lives, but creation of the conditions for self-management in mutual but voluntary co-operation with others. We urgently need to renew our understanding of the earlier ideal, which today is politically homeless.

The collapse of communism signalled the end of the 'age of collectivism', and collectivists are busy reformulating their ideals.[1] However, despite efforts to re-state their message in less economic terms, the political process continues to be the focus of their doctrine. For example, they typically call for more 'caring', but they measure the moral worth of individuals by the vehemence with which they demand that other people (the government) do something. Collectivists present their opponents as *un*caring, as if there were only two choices: *political* caring or *not* caring. But the yardstick is not how vigorously people call for the government to act, but their willingness to give of their own time and energy to help others.

Similarly, collectivists appeal to the human need for a sense of community or 'belonging' and they present their opponents as unconcerned about any such sentiment. But when collectivists speak of community they mean the political process. Moreover, the sense of belonging they advocate is that of followers under leadership. For the classical liberal, however, 'community' is no less important, but it does not imply a political obligation, rather it suggests a personal duty to set an example in the continuing struggle to uphold the moral and legal principles consistent with liberty. Thus, the new collectivism is about tapping into worthy sentiments—the desire to help, the desire to contribute to the common good, to belong—and politicising them.

Current party-political divisions still hark back to the old war of ideas between champions of a planned economy and a market economy. Today's challenge, however, is to understand the practical and moral limits of the political process, above all in the provision of health, education and welfare, where the political mind-set still dominates. Experience this century has surely taught us that political caring is a poor substitute for the mutual caring of civil society, and political solidarity an inadequate replacement for the sense of belonging that derives from free acceptance of a moral tradition to which all subscribe, rich and poor alike.

David G. Green

Summary

1 *Introduction*

- The welfare problem is not primarily financial but moral. The difficulty is not so much that the welfare state cannot be afforded, but that welfare programmes have tended to impair human character, above all by undermining the older ethos of 'community without politics'.
- Before the nationalisation of welfare, responsibility was divided three ways: there was, first, individual or family responsibility; second, the community as distinct from the state; and third, the government.
- Claiming benefit was considered to be 'letting the side down' and instead of expecting the government to provide assistance, the majority of the population assumed personal responsibility for fostering a 'public but not political domain' which cared for all those who were not able to support themselves.
- The crowding out of this tradition of concerted but non-political action for the common good has had two especially harmful moral effects.
    - First, it has rendered welfare services less effective in their central task of bringing out the best in people who are temporarily down on their luck. Consequently, instead of appealing to people's strengths the social security system panders to their weaknesses.
    - And second it has diminished opportunities for people to be of service to each other, impairing the quality of life and encouraging us to look outwards to 'the authorities', instead of inwards to our own strengths and skills, for solutions to shared problems.
- Is it possible to re-create today the tradition of non-political community service, once thought to be an indelible part of Britain's make-up?

2 *The Ideal of Liberty: A Re-statement*

- □ Liberty is not *'laissez faire'* or 'market forces', but is best understood as 'civil association' as distinct from 'corporate association'. A society of civil associates is based on three assumptions:
  - □ first, human nature at its best is about assuming personal responsibility both for self-improvement and making the world a better place for others;
  - □ second, people are seen to be united, not under leadership, but in acceptance of conditions which allow us all to exercise responsibility;
  - □ third government is understood to be the upholder of these conditions, that is, the conditions for liberty.
- □ A market economy is caricatured as the celebration of selfishness, whereas classical liberals from Adam Smith onwards understood liberty as a moral ideal. Nor is the market 'amoral'.
- □ A market system is morally educational in a workaday sense, but the market is not morally self-sufficient and its champions need to foster a moral order consistent with freedom.
- □ Three mistaken arguments advanced by some but not all free marketeers are criticised.
  - □ First, there is no 'natural right' to be free from all interference by the state. All actions of the state are not invasions of private rights.
  - □ Second, concern with morals is not inevitably 'authoritarian'. There can be responsibility without control; authority without commands; and respect for our common heritage without central direction. The moral order compatible with liberty is 'habitual' rather than 'intellectual'. It requires constant effort by everyone to uphold it. This dispersal of responsibility gives each

person important tasks to perform—everybody is somebody—and at the same time disperses those personal strengths and skills that help to guard against intrusive governments bent on imposing partisan doctrines.

- □ Third, hard-boiled economism, the doctrine that man can best be understood as a maximiser of his satisfactions, is mistaken. It neglects the importance of unthinking good habits and the ethos of self-improvement.

3 *Rationales for Collectivism*

□ Why has collectivism retained its vitality? Five rationales for collectivism are described and rebutted.

- □ The ideal of the medieval religious corporation provides part of the parentage of modern totalitarianism and retains a residual influence.
- □ The idea that the nation-state *is* an economy, rather than a social order which *has* an economy continues to provide inspiration for modern collectivists.
- □ Modern majoritarian democracy has corrupted the true democratic spirit. Modern elections serve to legitimise temporary absolute power. The higher ideal is to confine the political process to making laws that protect us all, and refraining from use of the political system to benefit one group at the expense of another. There are three problems: the political system has become a place where private interests bargain with governments for benefits; it has become more like a meeting of shareholders in a corporate enterprise, with national targets set for this or that and proposals put to the vote, with the outcome rarely in doubt; and law-making has increasingly became the issuing of mere management instructions.

□ Ten rationales for redistributive justice are discussed.

- The relief of poverty should not be confused with politically enforced equal outcomes.
- Merit can not be politically enforced. Enforcing equality at the starting gate undermines the family.
- The duty to assist the poor has been mingled with less worthy notions, including envy and the desire to profit at the expense of anonymous others.
- The deliberate confusion of freedom and power, by distinguishing between positive and negative freedom, is nothing but sophistry calculated to trick the unwary into surrendering their liberty in the name of freedom.
- Forcing the middle class into the state education and health systems does not raise general standards, but leads to middle-class capture.
- The claim that welfare should be universal as a badge of citizenship to unite people creates division rather than solidarity. Citizenship is desirable but the political process is not the only potential outlet. It intensifies the corruption of the vote-buying.
- Rawlsian theories are useful to collectivists because they muddy the water, falsely implying that it is possible to have a little bit of equality without a serious reduction in freedom.

- Claiming 'victim status' has become a popular strategy for winning political support for measures to gain advantages at the expense of others. But victim status undermines not only liberty, but also the self-respect of would-be victims.
- Corporate association appeals to two personality types: first, those who imagine they will be the leaders; and second, those who welcome the release from life's cares promised by the leaders. The tendency of such doctrines is to weaken human character by diminishing opportunities for us to develop our skills and our virtues through direct participation in overcoming the hazards of life.

- □ Civil association, by contrast, is intended to equip us for self-rule not political rule, that is, for non-political co-operation in joint endeavours. In doing so, it increases opportunities for service of others, whereas corporate association diminishes such opportunities and reduces our potential to grow as people, rendering us still more in need of paternalistic guidance.

4 *The Welfare System: What is Going Wrong?*

- □ Two approaches have emerged from the evolving American welfare debate: those who explain behaviour as the result of perverse incentives and those who contend that there has been cultural breakdown.
- □ Some British socialists, including the ethical socialists and Frank Field, are highlighting the harmful effects on character of aspects of modern collectivism.
- □ Britain is in the process of repeating American mistakes, leading to rising crime and family breakdown. Six intellectual errors bear special responsibility.
  - □ Behaviourism. Poor people are understood to be the victims of circumstance and the duty of government is to devise programmes to remedy their problem. The assumption that people react to outside stimuli which can be manipulated to bring about changes in their conduct provides a rationale for political paternalism.
  - □ Victimism. Poverty is considered to be the result of external forces which are unjust and entitle the victim to compensation. Not only does this view undermine personal responsibility by telling victims that they are incapable of solving their own problems, it provides a rationale for group hatred and demands for political discrimination.
  - □ Non-judgementalism. This mistaken doctrine derives largely from the belief that no one should be criticised because to do so is 'authoritarian'. But to praise or

blame one another is an inevitable part of the process of human growth and improvement.

- □ Resource rights. Freedom is precisely the ability to act within a legally-protected domain of initiative, but welfare rights are different. They are 'resource rights', or demands that political power be used to take the earnings or savings of one group for transfer to another. They are calls for other people to work or save in order that the holder of the right can live without necessarily working or saving. Protective rights, by comparison, are intended to give everyone a chance. They are mutual, whereas resource rights are confiscatory.

- □ Confusion of relief of poverty with equalisation. The intention of many public policies has not been primarily to relieve poverty, but to eradicate the unavoidable material reflections of human differences.

- □ Integrationism. Citizenship theorists, whether they label themselves one-nation Tories, one-nation Labour or social-democrats, argue that giving people spending power integrates them into the community, and that people are excluded from the community without spending power. This view assumes the solidarity of leader and led in corporate association, not the moral commitment and personal responsibility of civil association.

5 *Making A Reality of Civil Association*

□ Three requirements are suggested.

- □ We need to begin the de-politicisation of law making. This will involve constitutional reform to confine the state to its proper task of maintaining the conditions on which liberty rests.

- □ We need to restore a sense of personal responsibility and to rehabilitate virtue in its best sense.

- □ We need a positive campaign to restore tasks to civil society, that is to the domain of 'community without politics'. Governments should step back to create the space for a renewal of public but not political action; and second, they should refrain from actions which undermine personal responsibility, the family and voluntary associations.

□ Historically, a combination of a state minimum with the additional support of charities and mutual aid associations offered superior protection because it attended not only to cash needs but also to character. Support services should appeal to people's strengths, not their weaknesses.

□ There were two elements of Britain's philanthropic ethos.

- □ First, there was 'community without politics', a sense of solidarity with others that was based on an obligation to help others without degrading the recipient. Political solutions, by contrast, assume that lives are to be directed by the authorities and tend to be based on low expectations, with the result that people who are temporarily down on their luck are more likely to be 'locked-in' to their predicament.
- □ There was also a sense of 'duty without rights'. Everyone had a duty to help but no one had a right to receive assistance. Giver and receiver were both expected to take pains to show mutual respect. The modern mentality of welfare rights encourages people to demand whatever they can get away with.

6 *Some Policy Proposals*

□ There are two main rival approaches to reform.

- □ The present government's view is dismissed as indefensible.
- □ Second, the emerging socialist critique of Frank Field contends that means testing is the root cause of welfare

dependency. He argues that payments should be made as of right to provide an income floor on which people can build. Compulsory national insurance would be the norm and means testing kept to a minimum.

- The compulsory insurance advocated by Field is not sufficiently respectful of individual responsibility in two particular ways:
  - first, by requiring people to provide against contingencies through insurance it suppresses other methods, such as saving or capital investment, when it is from such diversity of provision that we learn better ways of meetings needs;
  - second, it fosters immaturity by encouraging reliance on the political authorities.
- National insurance assumes a relatively homogenous population of workers with a main job throughout life. This pattern is not longer the norm and new welfare systems should reflect the new variety of working lifestyles.
- Policy recommendations:
  - A genuinely independent voluntary sector should be encouraged by reducing the reliance of voluntary organisations on government grants. Increasing reliance has meant the steady infiltration of voluntary organisations by politicians and political concerns. Some voluntary associations have become lobbyists for taxpayer's money and others have ceased to play their traditional pioneering role because they are fearful of upsetting their political paymasters. A distinction should be made between registered voluntary organisations, which can receive government grants but do not benefit from tax concessions, and charities which rely 100 per cent on private finance.
  - Benefits which are insurable should be privatised.

National Insurance incapacity benefit and statutory sick pay should be abolished to allow private alternatives, including services offered by mutual aid associations, to emerge. Existing commitments should be honoured.

- Assistance of those able to work but out of work should be the shared responsibility of government and voluntary organisations. The Jobseekers Allowance is a step in the right direction, but the help given should be more personal.

- A new attitude should be encouraged. Instead of 'claim all you can get', income support should only be claimed as an absolute last resort. It should be a matter of honour to avoid claiming and to rely on savings wherever they exist. Consequently, it should be necessary to spend all capital, and all income should be deducted from benefit.

- Individuals should be able to avoid the more stringent means testing by opting to receive support from a voluntary association instead of the Benefits Agency. Voluntary organisations would be free to support individuals as they believed best, using their own money. Individuals opting for voluntary support, would not be legally required to spend their savings or have their earnings deducted from benefit. Such associations would concentrate on devising personalised schemes to help people back on their feet, and would need to be free to devise innovative policies. They would be able to arrange pathways back to independence through part-time work or training or personal morale-building without the benefit system producing perverse incentives. At present, a person on income support has no real reason to take part-time work. A face-to-face relationship with a voluntary association worker will not have the same corrupting effect because all assistance will be discretionary and subject to mutual agreement. In such a personal relationship, mutual respect, honour and good faith have a chance, but an arms-length relationship with a public official encourages dishonesty, bad faith and 'working the system'.

- Never-married mothers, but not divorced or widowed single parents, should be required to work as a condition of receiving benefit. Their benefits should not be cut, as Charles Murray and some American analysts contend, because to do so would cause too much hardship.

- Severe measures should be implemented to deter men from fathering illegitimate children. To father a child and to refuse to take responsibility should be marked out as one of the lowest things a man can do. Three new criminal offences should be introduced: failure by a father to register the birth of his child; threatening the mother with violence to conceal the father's identity; and failure to pay maintenance as ordered.

- At the turn of the century it used to be argued that the burden should be put on the woman to avoid pregnancy, because she would be least able to escape the consequences. This rationale no longer makes sense now that condoms are widely and cheaply available. It is a male responsibility to use a condom. The clear message the law should send is that any man contemplating sex outside marriage must be prepared to face the consequences of his actions.

- The Child Support Agency should confine its efforts to pursuing the fathers of illegitimate children, and responsibility for divorced men returned to the courts. The CSA should be an agency of the court not a department of government under political control.

1

Introduction

'Time's up for the welfare state'

THIS was the striking headline of a recent major article in *The Observer*, in which the distinguished left-leaning columnist Melanie Phillips, argued that socialists ought to re-think their commitment to the welfare state.[1] She is not alone. Socialist writer, David Selbourne has criticised the welfare state for encouraging a mentality of 'dutiless rights', and Labour MP Frank Field, Chairman of the House of Commons Social Security Committee, has criticised the social security system for encouraging dishonesty and undermining personal responsibility. In addition, 'ethical' socialists such as Professor A.H. Halsey and Norman Dennis have criticised the left for making egoistic demands on the state. Their voices have been added to those of classical-liberal writers like Charles Murray, who have long criticised the dependency-inducing effects of welfare.

Discussion of welfare reform is impaired by partisan political attachments, but both major political parties must share responsibility for its failings. The popular image of the Thatcher epoch is that the Government was intent on dismantling the welfare state, yet the reality of Thatcherism is that nothing remotely like dismantling took place. Indeed, the underlying trends either continued unabated or accelerated. Overall, welfare spending grew during the 1980s and welfare dependency increased. Welfare reform should not, therefore, be seen as a party-political issue. The welfare system is suffering from errors and misjudgments—some made much earlier this century and some made since the Second World War—whose damaging effects are only now being acknowledged, despite the endeavours of pioneering critics in the 1960s and 1970s.[2]

The study is organised as follows. First, in Chapter 2, I have tried to re-state the ideal of liberty. This re-statement is necessary because liberalism has become too closely associated in public debate with Thatcherism, whereas there has been a long tradition of liberty in Britain, stretching back many centuries. Thatcherism, with the perspective of time, will seem only a modest manifestation of it. Moreover, Thatcherism is the name of a party-political doctrine and was a compromise between liberal principles and the Tory paternalism which, historically, has often been at variance with liberty. Thatcherism was not the liberalism embodied in the tradition of thought represented by Locke, Smith, Tocqueville, Acton and Hayek.

Political parties are coalitions for capturing power and any philosophical tradition is bound to lose some of its consistency once it becomes a party instrument. During the Thatcher years, for instance, market language was often used to describe reforms, when the influence of market philosophy was either much attenuated or absent. The use of the term 'internal market' to describe the NHS reforms is probably the most striking example. It introduced a commercial spirit into the NHS which has served to enhance the effectiveness of rationing, without returning to consumers the power of choice taken from them by taxes. GP fundholders, for example are subject to market incentives devised to engineer outcomes. For Adam Smith and his followers, a competitive market is not a political device for manipulating individuals, but a means of liberating the best in people.

Chapter 2 also tries to refine some views touched upon, but not fully developed, in *Equalising People* (1990) and *Reinventing Civil Society* (1993). It examines some claims made by enthusiasts for economic freedom which, in reality, undermine liberty. In particular, I will argue that freedom should not be understood as liberation from obstacles to our wants, but should rather be seen as the exercise of personal responsibility. And personal responsibility implies two dispositions. On the one hand, it implies taking responsibility for progress and improvement—the 'vigorous virtues'[3]—and on the other hand it implies a duty to uphold established values and to measure up to inherited standards and expectations—the civic virtues. These dispositions are potentially divergent, but in practice they are mutually interdependent.

Chapter 3 asks why collectivism continues to enjoy support. It describes and rebuts the chief rationales for collectivism and their historical sources. This helps to put contemporary disputes into context and assists understanding of some modern lines of reasoning, including the new socialism.

Chapter 4 describes what is going wrong with the welfare system and Chapter 5 outlines the main elements of a free society and assesses the historical precedents for private welfare. It asks what, if anything, we can learn from the 19th century.

Chapter 6 puts forward some proposals, concentrating on social security and especially the relief of poverty. It argues that today's rule-bound social security has a deleterious effect on character, reinforcing human weaknesses rather than appealing to the best in people and calls for a more voluntary and discretionary system. There will be follow-up studies of health, education and pensions.

2

The Ideal of Liberty: A Re-Statement

IN HIS 1949 essay, *The Intellectuals and Socialism,* Hayek called for a renewal of Utopian liberal thought. What we lack, he said:

> is a liberal Utopia, a program which seems neither a mere defense of things as they are nor a diluted kind of socialism, but a truly liberal radicalism which does not spare the susceptibilities of the mighty ... which is not too severely practical, and which does not confine itself to what appears today as politically possible.[1]

Discovering how best to reform the welfare state is one of the biggest challenges now faced by classical liberals, and to do so, as Hayek recommended, by disregarding what is thought to be politically feasible in the short run remains as important as ever.

A glance at newspaper cuttings from the 1980s leaves an impression of welfare cuts and the 'dismantling' of services, but the actual record of welfare reform was abysmal. In truth, welfare spending grew during the Thatcher and Reagan years. The chief reason for the failure of market-inclined governments to reform welfare was the prevailing sense that it would be immoral to do so. Collectivists have successfully established in the public mind, not only that assistance of the poor is the moral responsibility of the government, but also that to demand more government welfare programmes is proof of compassion. There are two corollaries: first, that the more government welfare the individual demands the more worthy he is; and second, that anyone who doubts the value of the welfare state is morally *un*worthy. Free marketeers, contend the socialists, wish to 'dismantle' the welfare state because they do not care about the less fortunate. I will argue that planning to replace the welfare state, far from being proof of immorality, is necessary primarily for moral reasons. But first I must explain the moral philosophy typical of mainstream classical liberals and to identify some mistaken arguments sometimes associated with liberty.

Liberty as Civil Association

In *Reinventing Civil Society*, I followed the philosopher Michael Oakeshott in contending that modern European states can best be understood as torn between two divergent methods of association, and I have yet to find a better explanatory framework. The first type of association he calls 'civil association' and the second 'enterprise association'. The use of the term 'enterprise association' to describe collectivism struck some readers of the first draft of this chapter as counter-intuitive because 'enterprise' is usually taken to be desirable. Oakeshott's point is that, whilst *private* enterprise is desirable, it is dangerous for the state to act as if it were a private corporation. However, to avoid confusion, I will speak of 'corporate association' rather than Oakeshott's 'enterprise association'.

Each type of association is based on different assumptions about two other fundamental questions: the character of the people comprising the association (human nature); and the tasks and limits of government. Together, the principle of association, the conception of human nature and the attitude to the role of government constitute what Oakeshott calls the 'three inseparables'.[2] All political philosophies make assumptions about all three elements, whether explicitly or not.

A 'corporate association' is composed of persons united in pursuit of a common interest or objective. A nation might comprise many such corporate associations, including commercial companies, but here I am concerned with nation-states. In the pure form of a nation as a corporate association there is but one overriding national objective.

In a nation of 'civil associates' people are united not because they share a concrete goal, or are engaged together in a substantive task, but because they acknowledge the authority of the rules under which they live. Respect for the authority of the law does not imply that every person supports every law. The law changes and so what commands respect is both the law as it stands and the law-reforming process. People are united, not because they share the same wants, but because they accept that no person should exempt himself from the law as each pursues his own goals.[3] Each accepts the obligation to act justly towards others, and each enjoys equal status under the jurisdiction. This legal ethos is different from that in a corporate association. In both types of association people are subject to rules of conduct, but in a corporate association the rules are instrumental to the pursuit of the common aim. In the pure form of civil association, the laws are moral stipulations, not instrumental commands.[4]

The task of government under a corporate association is to manage the pursuit of the common goal and to direct individuals as appropriate. Individuals are seen primarily as performers of allotted tasks, under guidance. The task of the state under a civil association is to maintain and enforce the laws, and to supply services such as defence, which of necessity must be financed from taxation. The role of government is limited and under the law. Its task is not to manage people but to create the conditions in which people can freely associate for self-management.

Civil association also rests on a distinctive view of human nature. Individuals are seen, not as role players under leadership, but as intelligent agents understanding or not understanding their predicament, guided by beliefs, choices, sentiments or habits. This freedom is seen as a pleasure, not a burden. It is valued for its own sake, not only because it may lead to wanted outcomes. Indeed, it is taken to be what gives man dignity. The individual is autonomous, not isolated, that is, he has command of material resources and personal skills and acts in accordance with his self-conception, including an awareness of his own limits, and in pursuit of his own aims.[5] Individuals so conceived are the carriers of a moral compass: in short, each is a person with a character rather than an individual with a role.[6]

Thus, a civil association is not a mere collectivity of disparate individuals. It implies a strong bond of solidarity, but one very different from the unity typical of a corporate association. In a civil association the sense of solidarity of the people derives from the shared sense that the social system gives all of us a chance to do the best we can in our self-chosen sphere of life. No less important, it depends on awareness that the continuance of liberty rests on everyone doing his bit to uphold the personal virtues indispensable in a free society. The sense that we are all pulling our weight is a powerful unifying force.

The sense of solidarity in a corporate association, however, derives from the belief that each person is part of a single grand scheme, perhaps to modernise or develop the nation's resources or to mould human character in a new direction. Thus, in a nation organised as a corporate association, individuals are instruments of the government; whereas in a civil association the government is an instrument of the people, charged with keeping in good order the institutions which allow people to pursue their self-chosen ideals. But the individuals comprising a free society are united in a real sense. They cannot be understood as isolated individuals, a caricature that Hayek called the 'silliest of the common misunderstandings'.[7] The phrase 'civil association' stresses acceptance of shared conditions as the theme which unites people. Other scholars have made a similar point by emphasising that liberty is a word which describes a *process*, not an end result.[8] It is indeed a process, but Oakeshott's focus is more helpful in concentrating on what makes a free system work: namely the acceptance of shared conditions, legal and moral; the assumption of personal responsibility for maintaining them; and government which sees liberty, in the words of the second American president John Adams, as 'its end, its use, its designation, drift and scope', and no more.[9]

It is this conception of liberty as civil association that I will have in mind throughout this publication.

Classical Liberal Assumptions About Human Character and the Moral Order

One of the most powerful criticisms directed against enthusiasts for free markets is that they are immoral. In a variation of this argument, John Gray contends that a market system undermines the cultural foundations of society: the 'paleo-liberal celebration of consumer choice and market freedom as the only undisputed values has become a recipe for *anomie*, social breakdown and ultimately economic failure'.[10]

Thomas Carlyle, in *Past and Present*, published in 1843, set the tone of much later anti-capitalist rhetoric. His caricature of capitalism as based on the 'cash nexus' alone was embraced by Marx and is still mischievously repeated today. John Gray, for instance, refers to 'a view of society, explicit in Hayek and before him in Herbert Spencer, in which it is nothing but a nexus of market exchanges'.[11]

This caricature of liberty bears no resemblance to the arguments of classical-liberal writers such as Adam Smith, J.S. Mill, Tocqueville, Acton and Alfred Marshall, nor to modern champions, such as Hayek, Arthur Seldon and James Buchanan. Let me begin with an explanation of the views of Adam Smith on markets and morality.

Human beings, in Smith's view, were inclined to seek the approval of others, which meant that the greatest happiness came from acting in a manner considered virtuous and the greatest misery from infringing the moral expectations of other people. This tendency rested on 'sympathy', an emotion described in the opening sentence of *The Theory of Moral Sentiments:*

> How selfish soever man may be supposed, there are evidently some principles in his nature, which interest him in the fortune of others, and render their happiness necessary to him, though he derives nothing from it, except the pleasure of seeing it.[12]

What were the implications of this view for the design of the good society? Smith rejected the view, associated with Hobbes, that people are bad and that the only way to secure order is for the government to exercise control over them.

Law was necessary, in Smith's view, but the desire of men for praise meant that we could place considerable reliance on civil society for the maintenance of high moral standards.

But good conduct was not spontaneous. It had to be worked at by each individual struggling to be a better person and by each citizen taking an interest in the civil institutions which foster the best in people, notably the family and voluntary associations such as the church, charities or mutual aid associations. Smith believed there were three moral 'tribunals', the first two of which work with the grain of human nature:

> Nature, when she formed man for society, endowed him with an original desire to please, and an original aversion to offend his brethren. She taught him to feel pleasure in their favourable, and pain in their unfavourable regard.

But, he continues, the desire for approbation and the aversion to disapprobation does not alone make man fit for society. Accordingly, nature has endowed him, 'not only with a desire of being approved of, but with a desire of being what *ought* to be approved of'.[13]

The first tribunal was based on the desire for 'actual praise, and in the aversion to actual blame'; whereas the jurisdiction of the second—the 'man within'—was founded on the desire for:

> praiseworthiness, and in the aversion to blameworthiness; in the desire of possessing those qualities, and performing those actions, which we love and admire in other people; and in the dread of possessing those qualities, and performing those actions, which we hate and despise in other people.[14]

The term 'impartial spectator' is used repeatedly. Smith stressed the importance of the 'impartial and well-informed spectator' or 'the man within the breast', because he believed that people were inclined to over-value their own preferences. It was, therefore, important to take into account how others see us, because it makes us moderate our own beliefs and feelings, and temper our view of our own importance. The great law of Christianity, he says, is to love our neighbour as we love ourselves. And, he continues, 'it is the great precept of nature to love ourselves only as we love our neighbour, or, what comes to the same thing, as our neighbour is capable of loving us'.[15]

Smith's first tribunal may be understood as encouraging moral conformity; the second as promoting moral autonomy. Acton had also emphasised moral autonomy in his discussion of liberty: 'By liberty I mean the assurance that every man shall be protected in doing what he believes his duty against the influence of authority and majorities, custom and opinion.'[16]

According to Smith, there was also a third, 'still higher tribunal', that of the 'all-seeing Judge of the world, whose eye can never be deceived, and whose judgements can never be perverted'.[17]

This language may strike those only familiar with the Adam Smith of *The Wealth of Nations* as strange, but in his own day he was equally well known for *The Theory of Moral Sentiments*. He began as a moral philosopher, wrote *The Wealth of Nations* because of his concern to discover how best to release the majority of people from poverty, and returned to moral philosophy on completing it. *The Theory of Moral Sentiments* was his first book, originally published in 1759, and was revised constantly during his lifetime. There were six editions of the book and the final edition of 1790 was published only a year before his death. The alterations made to successive editions were substantial, whereas *The Wealth of Nations* underwent comparatively minor revision. The organisation of his lecture course at the University of Glasgow, where he was professor of moral philosophy, offers further insights. It was divided into four parts: natural theology, ethics, justice (or jurisprudence) and political expediency. The fourth part, on expediency, formed the basis of *The Wealth of Nations*. The third section on justice was intended to be a book, but remains available only as *Lectures on Jurisprudence*. The second section on ethics was the basis for *The Theory of Moral Sentiments*, which was also influenced by his lectures on natural theology.[18]

Smith's view is consistent with that of Aristotle. Moral goodness 'is the result of habit' and none of the moral virtues are natural, said Aristotle. They are engendered in us: 'neither *by* nor *contrary to* nature; we are constituted by nature to receive them, but their full development in us is due to habit'. In Aristotle's view, we acquire virtues by practising the activities that occasion them. People become builders by building, musicians by playing instruments and we become 'just by performing just acts, temperate by performing temperate ones, brave by performing brave ones'. So, he continues, 'it is a matter of no little importance what sort of habits we form from the earliest age—it makes a vast difference'. Good habits dispose us to act in just ways, hence, Aristotle says, the importance of having been trained 'from infancy to feel joy and grief at the right things'. True education is 'precisely this'.[19]

Such a morality demands a lot of the family, for it is in the family that children spend time with adults sufficiently committed to them to devote long hours to improving their character. For Adam Smith too, the family was fundamental. If it failed, he said, little could be done to make up for lost ground. Children went through a long period of dependence which required the support of both parents. This lengthy reliance of children on their parents was productive of the most salutary effects:

> During all this time the child being dependent on the parents is obliged in many instances to yield its will to theirs, to bring down its passions and curb its desires to such a pitch as they can go along with, and by this means learns in its very infancy a chief and most essential part of education.

Without learning to adjust to others, Smith thought, it is impossible for a person to 'have any peace or enjoyment in society'.[20] In keeping with his view that family life depends on regular close contact, he urged parents not to send their children away to boarding schools because, by living at home, 'Respect for you must always impose a very useful restraint upon their conduct; and respect for them may frequently impose no useless restraint upon your own'.[21]

James Q. Wilson has offered an updated assessment of Smith's views in the light of what the modern social and biological sciences have taught us. He argues that the modern challenge is to understand how best to nourish the moral sense identified by Smith. Some conservatives, says Wilson, argue that the schools should impress upon their pupils particular moral maxims and they take issue with leftists who argue that schools should 'clarify' the value choices the pupils might make. But, according to Wilson, children do not learn morality either by learning maxims or clarifying values:

> They enhance their natural sentiments by being regularly induced by families, friends, and institutions to behave in accord with the most obvious standards of right conduct—fair dealing, reasonable self-control, and personal honesty. A moral life is perfected by practice more than by precept; children are not taught so much as habituated. In this sense the schools inevitably teach morality, whether they intend to or not, by such behaviour as they reward or punish.[22]

And echoing Smith, he continues:

> We learn to cope with the people of this world because we learn to cope with the members of our family. Those who flee the family flee the world; bereft of the former's affection, tutelage, and challenges, they are unprepared for the latter's tests, judgements, and demands.[23]

But what should be made of Adam Smith's apparent endorsement of self-love? The observation that self-interest motivates people does not reflect cynicism, nor merely realism, on Smith's part. He believed, not only that it was perfectly proper for people to pursue their self-interest, but also pointed out that regard for others must always be built on self-interest because we have no other way of judging how others feel. The first precept of Christianity is 'to love the Lord our God with all our heart, with all our soul, and with all our strength, so it is the second to love our neighbour as we love ourselves'. And we love ourselves, he says, 'surely for our own sakes, and not merely because we are commanded to'.[24]

Smith believed that we can achieve much by pursuing our legitimate self-interest through mutual adjustment to others, but that any worthy human being should also seek to do right according to his sense of duty. According to Christian teaching, the sense of duty is not the 'sole' principle of our conduct, but it should be the 'ruling and the governing one', as both philosophy and common sense direct.[25] And Smith was in no doubt about where our duty lay:

> to feel much for others, and little for ourselves, that to restrain our selfish, and to indulge our benevolent, affections, constitutes the perfection of human nature; and can alone produce among mankind that harmony of sentiments and passions in which consists their whole grace and propriety.[26]

Thus, Smith did emphasise the importance of harnessing self-interest, but for him self-interest was not enough. We have a duty to pursue our self-interest unselfishly.

To sum up: Adam Smith's view of the good society, was one in which people took personal responsibility for making the world a better place. The law was there to mark out the sphere of personal responsibility and to foster the key institutions, such as the family. The central virtue was self-command. The major task for each generation in teaching the young was to encourage support for the good habits and duties which make life tolerable. But the whole edifice rested on the natural sociability of man, that is, on our innate moral sense.

Such were the arguments of Adam Smith. But liberals have not all followed Smith's lead. Allow me to identify three views, the first two of which are vulnerable to criticism and very different from Smith's line of reasoning. The first is that markets are morally neutral, and the second, that the market is morally self-sufficient. A third and more defensible argument is that the market is morally educational.

1. The Market is Amoral?

The first view treats the market as an exchange process which can be abstracted from its moral setting, a view I propose only to mention in passing. The historian Paul

Johnson has expressed it as clearly as anyone:

> I prefer to see the entrepreneurial spirit, of which capitalism is the result, not as positively virtuous, or for that matter as intrinsically sinful, but as morally neutral. It seems to me that capitalism is an impersonal force and therefore incapable of moral choices ... Focused solely on its own materialistic objectives, it has no room for idealism ... In a way it is like a marvellous natural computer. But it cannot make distinctions for which it is not programmed. Acutely responsive to market factors, it is blind to all others—blind to class, race, and color, to religion and sex, to nationality and creed, to good and evil.[27]

The blindness of market exchange to personal attributes can be one of its strengths, but competitive markets did, as a matter of historical record, emerge within a particular moral order and not elsewhere. Moreover, as I will argue below, it is dangerous to separate the system of voluntary exchange from its moral setting. To do so permits collectivists to argue that they can adopt the market technique for their own ends, namely to enjoy the prosperity it brings, without also embracing the personal responsibility and limited government with which it has historically been associated.

2. *The Market is Morally Self-Sufficient?*

Some enthusiasts for the market contend that the free play of enlightened self-interest produces an harmonious result. But is it enough to appeal to enlightened self-interest? One of the best discussions of this question can be found in *A Humane Economy* by Wilhelm Röpke, a close associate of Hayek and a founder member of the Mont Pelerin Society, whose resistance to the Nazis had led to him being forced out of his job at the University of Marburg in 1933.

The answer to the question, 'Is enlightened self-interest enough?' is 'decidedly in the negative', he says. For him, market ethics are on an intermediate plane: 'It is not the summit of heroes and saints ... selfless dedication, and contemplative calm, but neither is it the lowlands of open or concealed struggle in which force and cunning determine the victor and the vanquished.'[28]

Its ethical climate is lukewarm, but is favourable to an atmosphere of 'minimal consideration' for others and 'a certain correspondence of give and take', quite apart from its encouragement of productive energy. This energy is applied 'not in building pyramids for the glory of emperors, but to improving the well-being of the masses'. Even if we find only bare material advantage, the man who decently provides for himself and his family does no mean thing. His is a higher morality than that of those who pride themselves on their generosity at others' expense. But Röpke does not conclude that the market is self-sufficient. He is intolerant of 'economically ignorant moralism' which 'always wills the good and works the bad', but he equally repudiates 'morally callous economism'.[29] The market economy, he says, is not enough. Economic life does not go on in a moral vacuum. It is constantly in danger of 'straying from the ethical middle level unless it is buttressed by strong moral supports' which 'must simply be there' and, no less important, must 'constantly be impregnated against rot'. Otherwise, any free economic system must ultimately collapse.[30] Lest his view is in doubt, he says:

> The market, competition, and the play of supply and demand do not create these ethical reserves; they presuppose them and consume them. These reserves have to come from outside the market ... Self-discipline, a sense of justice, honesty, fairness, chivalry, moderation, public spirit, respect for human dignity, firm ethical norms—all of these are things which people must possess before they go to market and compete with each other. These are the indispensable supports which preserve both market and competition from degeneration.[31]

Frank Knight, founder of the Chicago school, took a not dissimilar view. Business behaviour, he said, ought to be constrained by moral limits. There is much truth, said Knight, in the idea that the desire to 'get ahead', and especially to 'get ahead of other people, is the primary sin to be avoided'.[32]

For economists not to recognise these obvious truths is fatal, argued Röpke: 'The market's asymmetry opens a gap which has to be closed from without, from beyond the market, and it would be sheer suicide on the part of the market economy's friends to leave to others the cheap triumph of this discovery.'[33]

3. *The Market is Morally Educational?*

Röpke argued vigorously against the self-sufficiency of enlightened self-interest, but defended the educational role of competition. The market and competition are far from generating their moral pre-requisites autonomously, but within a framework of law, a market economy tends to encourage openness and certain workaday values, such as 'honesty is the best policy'. Compared with a political system in which unfettered power is exercised, or contrasted with monopoly, competition increases the chances of being caught and to that extent encourages good conduct. Its educational value should not, therefore, be diminished. Tocqueville's view was similar. American preachers in the 1830s taught 'self-interest rightly understood', an ethos that demanded fewer acts of romantic self-sacrifice but suggested daily small acts of self-denial: it disciplined persons in habits of regularity, temperance, moderation, foresight, and self-command.[34]

To sum up, we can credit capitalism, the market, competition, voluntary exchange, the system of natural liberty, the play of supply and demand—however the system is characterised—with educational influences. Moreover, voluntary exchange is based on trade by mutual consent rather than force. It is based, therefore, on respect for other people and this alone is a powerful argument in its favour. But there is more.

Despite these qualifications, the claim that free marketeers foster selfishness finds no support in the writings of the leading classical liberal thinkers. Nor can it rightly be claimed that a market economy automatically undermines the moral order. From Adam Smith onwards there has been a rich tradition of writing about the moral underpinnings of liberty.

Three Arguments That Play Into the Hands of Collectivism

Before turning to the rationales for corporate association, I must first deal with three arguments, commonly deployed by friends of liberty, which are not consistent with the view I am taking and which, if widely accepted, would make it impossible to erect the rationale for reform I am advocating.

1. Belief in Innate Goodness

Some libertarians build their case for freedom on the 'natural right' to be free from all interference. People are assumed to have certain innate qualities which will shine forth if the government gets out of the way. This is how Rousseau put it:

> compassion is a natural feeling, which by moderating the activity of love of self in each individual, contributes to the preservation of the whole species. It is this compassion that hurries us without reflection to the relief of those who are in distress: it is this which in a state of nature supplies the place of laws, morals, and virtues.[35]

Superficially Rousseau may seem to be advancing the same argument as Smith. However, Smith thought that 'sympathy' was the basis of virtue, not a substitute for it. According to the view taken by Rousseau, all influences from outside the individual should be treated with suspicion as invasions of rights. Even the weight of opinion is so regarded, an attitude in sharp contrast to that of Adam Smith. Smith's argument was not that we should sweep away institutions to set loose raw nature. His fundamental concern was to understand how best to nourish the institutions which worked with the grain of human nature.

As Adam Smith taught, we are social animals and, therefore, our attitudes, habits and dispositions—our nature, for practical purposes—reflect the institutions which make up a society. There is no core human nature we can get back to, because we can never eradicate all the influences upon us. The human condition *is* social. This is also Hayek's argument when he observes that the moral order at any moment is the product of an evolutionary process.[36]

As Hayek pointed out, the very concepts we use to express our ideas have evolved over time. They emerge from political, economic and social circumstances. Some natural-rights theorists, however, postulate a pre-existing world. They attempt to 'start again' from scratch by imagining what people are 'really' like. But they over-estimate their capacity to stand aside from the world. As Hayek argued, the ideas contained in our brains are not fully our own because they are part of the common heritage which has evolved over many centuries.[37]

Some defenders of 'natural rights' seem to treat every action by the state as subtracting from the total of potential individual actions. This view fails to recognise that rights require enforcement and that even to conceive of rights presupposes an enforcement agency. Not every scholar who has spoken of natural rights believed that there could be rights without law. William Blackstone, for instance, referred to natural rights, but he plainly understood that law was central to liberty.[38] As Hayek argued, the Western tradition of freedom has been concerned with the creation of a personal domain protected by law. The state ensures that individuals are secure in what they earn and that lawful agreements will be enforced, and leaves them otherwise free to bring about improvements as they believe best. As Adam Smith put it:

> Commerce and manufactures can seldom flourish long in any state which does not enjoy a regular administration of justice, in which the people do not feel themselves secure in the possession of their property, in which the faith of contracts is not supported by law, and in which the authority of the state is not supposed to be regularly employed in enforcing the payment of debts from all those who are able to pay.[39]

He repeatedly stressed the importance of law. The factor which contributes above all to prosperity is, he said:

> that equal and impartial administration of justice which renders the rights of the meanest British subject respectable to the greatest, and which, by securing to every man the fruits of his own industry, gives the greatest and most effectual encouragement to every sort of industry.[40]

Some natural rights theorists do not fully recognise that rights assume the presence of law and have no reality without it. It is, of course, possible to argue without self-contradiction that a particular right *should* be recognised in law. The American campaigners for independence used the language of natural rights to defend their resistance to the imposition of an unjust tax. Their concern, like that of an earlier generation of English writers including Locke, was to justify rebellion against the established order in the name of higher moral code. Locke was concerned to make the moral case for deposing an unjust king, James II, and the American revolutionaries for severing their connection with George III. They appealed to natural rights to assert that there were higher moral principles than those acknowledged by the powers that be. Against that view there is no argument, but it asserts that human affairs should be guided by a higher morality; a contention very different from the claim inherent in Rousseau's argument quoted earlier (p. 17) that both legal requirements and moral principles alike are invasions of individual freedom. Such a view recognises no moral claims on individual conduct, but asserts the superiority of personal (natural) preferences.

2. *Concern With Morals is Authoritarian*

Closely associated with natural rights theories is the claim that it is authoritarian to raise moral issues. The reasoning goes something like this. The champion of liberty should be consistent; he should be against coercion of all types; all morals are coercive and, therefore, the true believer in freedom should not moralise. There should be no control of the economy by government and no control of personal lifestyles. Such libertarians appear to believe that all values should be personal. Of course, some libertarians favour leading a moral life, but they insist that it is for everyone to choose his own good life. We are each equal judges of what is good or right.

A libertarian capitalist view has been consistently advocated by Samuel Brittan since the 1960s, first in *Left or Right:*

The Bogus Dilemma (1968), then in *Capitalism and the Permissive Society* (1973), *A Re-Statement of Economic Liberalism* (1988) and *Capitalism With a Human Face* (1995). Thatcherite economic policies, says Samuel Brittan, took place against a background of 'obsessive secrecy, petty authoritarianism and a highly illiberal rhetoric on social and personal issues'. He cites a US survey which discovered that 'moral conservatives' saw divorce, co-habitation, homosexuality and abortion as evidence of 'moral decay', whilst libertarians believed they showed 'greater social tolerance'.[41] Brittan's sympathies lie with the libertarians. Assessing the Thatcher years up to mid-1987 he writes:

> There is more understanding of markets as a form of co-ordination superior to collectivist compulsion. But belief in personal freedom, on which the ultimate justification of the whole approach rests, has taken some knocks, which I hope will prove temporary. People may make many mistakes in the use of freedom, and nature or society may have many unforeseen snags in store. But in the end the dangers from freedom are far, far less than the dangers from heeding those on the left and right who deign to tell their fellow citizens how to live.

He proceeds to lump together 'moral authoritarians' and 'economic collectivists' whom he finds guilty of 'arrogance' and 'absurdities'.[42]

Adherents of this line of reasoning sometimes contrast the 1980s free marketeers with those of the 1990s. In the 1980s, it is said, the New Right meant free markets plus free lifestyles, whereas increasingly in the 1990s free marketeers are combining a commitment to a competitive market economy with attachment to moral virtue. William Bennett's *The Book of Virtues*,[43] exemplifies this trend in the US, where it has become a best seller.

Thus, some libertarians object to the linking of markets and morals, claiming that to do so is authoritarian. Their mistake is to fail to distinguish between external control and internal self-restraint. Internal restraint does mean measuring up to standards which are not purely personal. Accepted codes of behaviour are part of the cultural heritage which is our lot at birth. Some libertarians, however, see no difference between, on the one hand, measuring up to an inherited standard, such as the Christian tradition and, on the other, being controlled by someone. They object to any effort to pressurise someone into right conduct. Samuel Brittan, quoted above, speaks of 'deigning' to tell people what to do. But the person who advocates virtue or good character need not be 'telling' anybody anything. He offers a view of the good life for others to accept or reject. But he does *offer* it and he may offer it vigorously, but that is quite different from imposing it.

Some libertarians insist that it is repressive, even unhealthy, to restrain instincts. Adam Smith was in no doubt that self-command was fundamental: 'Self-command is not only itself a great virtue, but from it all the other virtues seem to derive their principal lustre'.[44] But the self-restraint he had in mind was very different from the annihilation of instincts recommended by some in the early Christian tradition. Efforts to annihilate, rather than restrain, natural desires have typically led to pre-occupation with the next world, perhaps in the manner of monks and hermits, or in some cases in the guise of (real) authoritarianism.

When speaking of morals, libertarians think in terms of two categories: government and individual. And the government, they say, should not dictate morals. Consequently, they are reluctant to engage in moral criticism because they believe that to do so is to open up a role for government. They disregard the third category of culture or community and a sense that we have a *shared* responsibility for the moral order, not under the leadership of government. They are right to worry about the government stipulating a new morality, but wrong to think that, therefore, we must leave it to individuals acting alone. As Tocqueville warned, a powerful state is content that people should think of nothing but pleasure, in order that the élite is left free to rule.

Nobel-prize winner Professor James Buchanan wrote in the mid-1970s about the danger of neglecting the moral basis of freedom: 'those of us who do sense the vulnerability of social order to what seem to us to be gradual but unmistakable changes in the moral bases of this order would be derelict in our own duty if we did not raise warning flags.' The problem of social order is faced eternally, he says, by men who realize that to live together 'they must impose *upon themselves* social rules'. Economists 'cannot evade their responsibility in the continuing discourse over such rules and institutions'.[45]

Hayek also recognised the centrality of moral order. In his final book, *The Fatal Conceit,* he offers an evolutionary explanation for human culture, stressing how freedom rests on a moral framework, and arguing that the virtues essential to a free society, 'are not transmitted automatically'.[46] We must take pains, he says, to pass our values from generation to generation through teaching, historically a task carried out by churches. He singles out private or 'several' property and the family as the main institutions that have shaped and furthered Western civilisation.[47] Hayek had also emphasised the importance of religious movements during his address to the first meeting of the Mont Pelerin Society in 1947. He went so far as to say that, unless the breach between 'true liberal and religious convictions' could be healed, there was 'no hope for a revival of liberal forces'.[48]

But what should classical liberals make of the libertarian counter culture? In *The Dream and the Nightmare* Myron Magnet lambasts the champions of American counter-culture, whose doctrines have become entangled with support for the welfare state.

Collectivist intellectuals sought two liberations, one for themselves, and one for the 'Have-Nots'. First, the War on Poverty, school busing and affirmative action were intended to 'liberate' the black and poor from their poverty. And second, the 'Haves' sought to liberate themselves from convention. According to the counter-culture, America was guilt-ridden and materialistic, its surface sobriety hypocritical and the family, coercive.[49] The ideal was to drop out and become a guilt-free, whole, undivided person. According to Magnet, the cultural revolution linked this quest for personal liberations for the Haves with political liberation for the Have-Nots. In doing so: 'It dignified the purely personal, making self-cherishing seem unselfish, almost civic-minded'.[50]

This attitude made it especially hard for adherents to confront the failure of policies which gave them their sense of self-esteem. The result has been defence of racial quotas, excusing criminals as victims rather than wrongdoers, and uncritical support of never-married mothers regardless of how well they are bringing up their children. In other words, morally indefensible polices came to be defended with moral zeal.[51]

The consequence has been what Americans have came to call the underclass, whose poverty has become entrenched because the ideology of libertarian collectivists celebrates self-destructive behaviour.[52] They could have learnt from Adam Smith, who had warned two centuries earlier of the catastrophic results for the poor of moral laxity:

> The vices of levity are always ruinous to the common people, and a single week's thoughtlessness and dissipation is often sufficient to undo a poor workman for ever, and to drive him through despair upon committing the most enormous crimes. The wiser and better sort of the common people, therefore, have always the utmost abhorrence and detestation of such excesses, which their experience tells them are so immediately fatal to people of their condition.

It was different for the rich, said Smith. Extravagance or laxity might not ruin 'a man of fashion', and people of that rank were apt to consider indulgence or excess as one of the privileges of their wealth.[53] Adam Smith, however, was not on the reading list of the leaders of American counter-culture.

To sum up: as Adam Smith and mainstream classical liberals understood, a free society depends on personal responsibility. That is, it depends on virtue; and virtue is nourished in the family and in voluntary associations. For the libertarian-collectivist élite, the family is a source of guilt-stained hypocritical moral codes and should be dispensed with, and the responsibilities of voluntary welfare associations should be assumed by the state.

The argument of libertarian free marketeers like Samuel Brittan is directed at leftist enthusiasts for freedom of lifestyle. He urges them to hang on to their desire to be liberated from 'authoritarian' moral codes, but at the same time to abandon their desire for the government to control personal spending on health, education and pensions. To be consistent, he says, they should demand free lifestyles and freedom from government control of personal expenditure.

His argument seems to be that if they want freedom from *one* constraint, they should also want freedom from *all* constraints. In essence he accepts the underlying philosophical premise of the libertarian-collectivist intelligentsia. He does not embrace their wish to transfer wealth from the rich to the poor, but he does share their underlying error, namely their mistaken and egoistic view of freedom as power. As Hayek argued, it is dangerous to define freedom as 'the absence of obstacles to the realisation of our desires', as Bertrand Russell did, or to claim that 'liberty is power, the effective power to do specific things', as John Dewey and his followers did.[54] This confusion has been fostered as part of the campaign for socialism, but once this identification of freedom with power is admitted, says Hayek, 'there is no limit to the sophisms by which the attractions of the word "liberty" can be used to support measures which destroy individual liberty', and no end to the tricks by which people can be 'exhorted in the name of liberty to give up their liberty'.[55]

This, however, is precisely the confusion which explains the ideology of the libertarian collectivists who link, on the one hand, freedom from moral restraint with, on the other, freedom (for the poor) from wanting material goods they can not afford. And it is also the trap into which libertarian free marketeers like Brittan have fallen. He wants freedom from (some but not all) moral restraints and freedom from (some but not all) government controls. Yet, it is an inescapable part of the human condition to grow to adulthood within a cultural heritage which, in every society so far known to history, has taken a view about matters such as the family and the obligations owed by biological parents to their own children. To label efforts to uphold a given moral view as 'authoritarian' ignores the inevitability of shared moral concern in any social order and telescopes the valid distinction between the *external* enforcement of standards and *self*-control in the light of the moral tradition into which we are born.

Toleration and Taboo

But let me, even at the risk of labouring the point, persist a little further in trying to understand the moral climate that is consistent with, and necessary to, a free society. For; it must be conceded that there is a sense in which a morality, though not strictly coercive, might be suffocating and therefore of legitimate concern.

Again, Oakeshott has captured the essence of the problem. Morality, he says (in the tradition of Aristotle), can be 'practical' or 'intellectual'. An 'intellectual' moral system erects rules or ideals to guide conduct. A certain amount of difficulty arises because the ideals are abstractions, so that there is a constant problem of how to apply them in practice. But a particular weakness of an intellectual morality, says Oakeshott, is that it tends to require 'perfection as the crow flies', particularly where it is embodied in the form of an ideal rather than a rule. His point is that the pursuit of righteousness has been known to harden many a heart. We can, for example, see this contradiction in those political activists who pursue with passion the ideal of 'social justice', whilst having no command of the ordinary face-to-face decencies.[56] Moral behaviour, says Oakeshott, is conduct to which there is an alternative, but this does not mean that a conscious choice must always be made. A man may act morally out of habit, and his conduct may be recognisably good or bad, despite his lack of reflection.[57]

It is this 'practical' or habit-based morality that is consistent with civil association, because it is evolving and tolerant of defiance. It offers a clear view about right and wrong, so that children can be given unequivocal guidance, but it can change with circumstances and avoids the danger of rigidity.

But Oakeshott's interpretation of habitual moral systems is not the most prevalent among classical liberals. Habitual moralities are associated with superstition, but we should not over-estimate the tendency of habitual moral systems to degenerate into taboo. As Oakeshott writes:

> the appearance of changelessness in a morality of traditional behaviour is an illusion which springs from the erroneous belief that the only significant change is that which is either induced by self-conscious activity or is, at least, observed on the occasion. The sort of change which belongs to this form of the moral life is analogous to the change to which a living language is subject: nothing is more habitual or customary than our ways of speech, and nothing is more continuously invaded by change.[58]

Moreover, intellectual moral systems substitute their own rigidity, that of doctrinal purity. A good measure of the tolerance and adaptability of a moral system is its attitude to eccentrics. Moral eccentricity, says Oakeshott, is of value to a society whose morality is one of habit of behaviour. Within an habitual moral system the attitude to moral eccentricity is ambiguous. It is: 'admired but not copied, reverenced but not followed, welcomed but ostracized'.[59] In a system based on ideals formulated in words, precisely because of the constant negotiation and re-negotiation of the wording of the ideals and their application, defiance has a tendency to be less welcome.

We need to renew our understanding of the tolerant, adaptive moral system which leaves room for the eccentric. A morality for freedom should offer a clear guide to conduct against which we can judge ourselves, and there must be tolerance of defiance and tolerance of critics of defiance. If the moral system most appropriate to a free society is habitual, then the importance of the family and other intermediate associations becomes easier to see. An habitual morality is essentially a practical way of living which is learnt or acquired by copying or emulating others. No moral system is ever purely devoid of reflection, nor could it be, but moral systems—in the same manner as language—work well without the participants being able to articulate the rules governing their conduct, just as most people can not articulate the grammatical rules they follow when speaking. In this manner parents use stories to convey moral truths to their children. To explain a moral principle in the abstract is difficult, but to tell a story with a 'moral' to it has proved far more effective.

Above all, such a moral system is the possession of the people, that is of civil society. It stands or falls by the efforts of each person going about his daily life, upholding or not upholding the virtues it embodies. Everyone counts. And this is its relevance for liberty. Because such a moral system rests on daily face-to-face practice, it is less prone to manipulation by the authorities. Typically authoritarian governments bent on re-moralising their people have formulated their morals as ideals and sought to impose righteousness. Communism certainly assumed this character, as did the Islamic fundamentalism which followed the overthrow of the Shah of Iran. A people wishing to be free should nourish those institutions which foster the practical morals that guide conduct whilst simultaneously remaining open to influence. It is no coincidence that modern tyrannies, from the French Revolution through to twentieth-century fascism and communism, have sought to reduce the influence of, not only the family, but also the voluntary associations which nourish virtue and give individuals the unified strength to resist the unwelcome intrusions of governments that would exceed those proper but limited duties necessary to uphold liberty.

Libertarians (above p. 22) contend that no one should criticise lifestyle choices of certain kinds (in practice mainly to do with sex and the family) but they have lost the sense that it is mutually respectful to be part of a community in which we each help each other to discover what is right through our demonstrations of approval or disapproval. We need to re-learn older attitudes reflected in outdated words such as chiding, upbraiding, rebuking and reproaching. These imply the gentle disapproval of a father or mother towards a much-loved son or daughter, rather than the stern or harsh censure of the Dickensian schoolmaster with cane in hand. The state of mind of the would-be critic or upholder of values is not 'moral dudgeon' but sadness combined with that sympathy for the wrongdoer that flows from knowledge of one's own weaknesses.

Finally to summarise: the idea underlying the censure of the self-styled anti-authoritarians is that man is naturally good and that, consequently, we need to clear the way for nature. However, as Aristotle and Adam Smith understood, nature prepares us for morality, but does not supply us with a ready-made product. Individuals are communal creatures. Our moral system is a shared responsibility, but this recognition does not imply leadership or control. There can be responsibility without control; authority without commands; and respect for our common heritage without central direction.

3. *Hard-Boiled Economism: Man as a Rational Satisfaction Seeker*

I turn now to a related question which has got me into a certain amount of hot water with some of my friends. In *Reinventing Civil Society* I criticised 'hard-boiled economism', the name I gave to a set of assumptions about human nature employed by some, but by no means all, economists. I have in mind those who present economics as the study of rational economic calculation. I should say that this is also a self-criticism, for in some of my earlier work I partly adopted the approach I later came to criticise.

Professor Gary Becker has stated the hard-boiled view as clearly as anyone. He holds that the economic approach is applicable to all human behaviour:

> The heart of my argument is that human behaviour is not compartmentalised, sometimes based on maximising, sometimes not, sometimes motivated by stable preferences, sometimes by volatile ones, sometimes resulting in an optimal accumulation of information, sometimes not. Rather, all human behaviour can be

> viewed as involving participants who maximise their utility from a stable set of preferences and accumulate an optimal amount of information and other inputs in a variety of markets.[60]

He applies these assumptions across the board, but perhaps most famously to the study of marriage:

> According to the economic approach, a person decides to marry when the utility expected from marriage exceeds that expected from remaining single or from additional search for a more suitable mate... Similarly, a married person terminates his (or her) marriage when the utility anticipated from becoming single or marrying someone else exceeds the loss in utility from separation, including losses due to physical separation from one's children, division of joint assets, legal fees, and so forth.[61]

Hard-boiled economism is mainly a pre-occupation with scientific study, that is it concentrates on what can be quantified and leaves the rest out. Many economists feel they have to be useful to business leaders and governments and that consequently they must attempt to make predictions. Leading contributors to economic theory, such as Gordon Tullock, co-founder of the public choice school, know perfectly well that they simplify human motivation as a matter of methodological convenience.

Tullock discusses some of the dilemmas of the hard-boiled perspective in his IEA study, *The Vote Motive*:

> If bureaucrats are ordinary men, they will make most of (not all) their decisions in terms of what benefits them, not society as a whole. Like other men, they may occasionally sacrifice their own well-being for the wider good, but we should expect this to be exceptional behaviour.

The theory of bureaucracy, he says, should therefore:

> be based upon the assumption that bureaucrats are as self-seeking as businessmen, and it should concern itself with the design of constraints which will make the bureaucrats' self-interest identical with the interests of society.

And what are the motivations of bureaucrats? What are their interests? Bureaucrats try to improve their own utility, which:

> like everyone else's, is partly based upon their immediate ability to consume goods and partly on their appreciation of good things

> happening to other people. In other words, they are partly selfish and partly public interested.[62]

One of the advantages of the simple profit-maximising assumption economists use to study business is that it permits them to assume a single 'maximand' (something a person is trying to maximise) and make calculations. Tullock continues:

> if we consider the businessman as maximising his utility —Marshall's net advantages—we no longer have as easy a problem. His utility is, to him, a simple 'function' which he can maximise; but, to us as outsiders, what is observed is a number of different elements, such as his income, respect in his profession, the beauty of his secretary, other aspects of his office, etc. We would have to work out a complex function of all those variables and then attempt to maximise it; and this complex function would have to be identical to the one he uses in utility maximising.

As a result of this complexity economists have tended to assume a simple, single goal: profit. There is a loss of accuracy, Tullock concedes, but it is 'fortunately slight'.[63]

Is there, he asks, a similar maximand we can use for bureaucracies? The answer is, unfortunately 'No', if the economist wants to formulate general laws. But, if economists confine their studies to the type of bureaucracy typical of Western countries, there is a simple criterion similar to 'profit', namely the 'size of the bureaucracy'. We can 'Assume the bureaucrats are simply attempting to maximise the size of their bureaucracies and leave aside, for the time being, their desire to consume leisure'. Economists, he says, have achieved many insights with their simple, one-argument 'utility function' for businessmen (profit-maximisation) and though he does not expect so much progress from size-maximisation, at least he says 'we should make some progress'.[64]

Tullock, therefore, is conscious that he is simplifying human motivations, but because of his concern with the possibility of calculation and prediction, maintains that analysis based on a simple maximand is useful. In practice, however, some economists forget the limitations and treat people as self-serving calculators *per se*. They adopt what Ralph Harris sometimes calls a 'cash-register' view of human nature.

But Adam Smith did not look upon people purely as utility maximisers (with either a broad or a narrow utility function). Nor did Marshall. Neither did Hayek. And nor did other modern economists like Röpke, who pulled no punches in their censure of socialism in all its strains. A particular disadvantage of hard-boiled economism, despite its obvious fruitfulness in analysing some types of behaviour, is that it can divert our attention from problems which are more urgent. As Frank Knight, founder of the Chicago school, argued:

> The idea that the social problem is essentially or primarily economic, in the sense that social action may be concentrated on the economic aspect and other aspects left to take care of themselves, is a fallacy, and to outgrow this fallacy is one of the conditions of progress toward a real solution of the social problem as a whole, including the economic aspect itself.[65]

And James Buchanan, in the foreword to a modern edition of Frank Knight's *Freedom and Reform*, has written that Knight would have regarded the re-emergence of 'Old-fashioned *homo economicus*, or man as net-wealth maximizer', as reflecting 'retrogression into a simplistic and wrongheaded usage of the valuable insights that economic theory can offer'. Buchanan continues:

> *Home economicus* exists in every man, but one of Knight's most persistent themes through all his works is that there exist all sorts of other men (the romantic fool, the sportsman who enjoys the fray, the prejudiced ignoramus, the man who wants to be a 'better' man) alongside the rational maximizer of economic interest.[66]

In another work, Professor Buchanan warns against the tendency of economic theory to 'force all analysable behaviour' into the straitjacket of 'maximising a utility or objective function under constraints'.[67]

The economic approach to crime provides an example. It is generally a significant improvement on the sociological approach, which typically offers deterministic explanations of criminal activity, including accounts which attribute causal influence to poverty, unemployment or genetic make-up. The economic approach, by contrast, treats crime as a choice made after calculation of the likely gain or loss from an anticipated criminal act compared with any alternative activity. A perception that a given criminal act is very likely to lead to capture, for instance, would deter a potential criminal, as might an increase in the severity of sentencing.

But this style of reasoning does not explain why some people would not commit a crime even if they thought there was a low chance of being caught and that the punishment would be negligible in the rare event of their being detected. Many people have been brought up to do the right thing, even though no one is looking. That is, they have been trained in good habits. They do not make a conscious choice not to commit a crime. For them, crime is literally 'unthinkable'. Most readers of this book, I dare say, would not break into their neighbours' house to steal their video, even if they felt certain they would get away with it. A theory accounting for crime should, therefore, embrace not only the assumption that potential criminals calculate the risks involved in choosing between criminal and non-criminal actions, but also the functioning of those institutions which instil unthinking good habits, not least the family.

The model of man as a satisfaction seeker, not only has difficulty accounting for man as a follower of unreflective good habits, but also man as a self-improving character. As James Buchanan writes: 'Man does not want liberty in order to maximise his utility, or that of the society of which he is part. He wants liberty to become the man he wants to become.'[68] Man is both 'natural and artifactual', says Buchanan, because we are the products of both a cultural heritage and our own efforts to become better than we are.[69] By refusing to see man as 'artifactual' we neglect both the 'constitution of private man' (or 'character') and also the 'constitution of public men', that is, the 'character' or moral underpinning of a free society.[70]

As Röpke also saw, there is danger in allowing economic freedom to be separated from its moral environment. To speak of the 'price mechanism' is perfectly legitimate, he said, so long as we remember that 'we have narrowed our angle of vision and do not forget that the market economy is the economic order proper to a definite social structure and to a definite spiritual and moral setting'. The sphere of the market may be regarded and defended 'only as part of a wider general order encompassing ethics, law, the natural condition of life and happiness, the state, politics and power'. To forget this truth is to be guilty of social rationalism which misleads us into 'imagining that the market economy is no more than an 'economic technique' that is applicable in any kind of society and in any kind of spiritual and social climate'.[71] And to treat the economy as such a technique is precisely the error made by socialists who believe the price mechanism can be used by them. But, asks Röpke: 'How could a genuine market, an area of freedom, spontaneity, and unregimented order, thrive in a social system which is the exact opposite in all respects?'[72]

There is another sense in which some economists have played into the hands of socialists. It is, in the view of Röpke, by embracing what he calls the 'cult of the standard of living'. He criticises three ideas: economism, materialism and utilitarianism.[73] It is economism:

> to allow material gain to obscure the danger that we may forfeit liberty, variety, and justice and that the concentration of power may grow, and it is also economism to forget that people do not live by cheaper vacuum cleaners alone but by other and higher things which may wither in the shadow of giant industries and monopolies. To take one example among many, nowhere are the economies of scale larger than in the newspaper industry, and if only a few press lords survive, they can certainly sell a maximum of printed paper at a minimum of pennies or cents; but surely the question arises of what there is to read in these papers and what such an accumulation of power signifies for freedom and culture.[74]

By 'materialism' he means 'an attitude which misleads us into directing the full weight of our thought, endeavour, and action towards the satisfaction of sensual wants'. It is linked to utilitarianism, that is applying a single scale of values, and failing to recognise some as higher than others. He recalls Pascal's dictum that man's dignity resides in thought. In the post-war world he complained, it had resided in the standard of living.[75]

Röpke was writing in 1958, when few imagined that the collapse of communism would be possible. He feared that the 'cult of productivity' weakened the West in its battle against communism, a conflict which could only be won on moral grounds. Moreover, he thought it sowed the seeds of totalitarianism, which in Germany had prospered because of the loss of moral bearings. His warning has heightened value because he had lived through the rise of Hitler who he believed had prospered, in part, because champions of liberty had failed to defend capitalism as a moral system. Totalitarianism is an 'infernal mixture of unbridled power and deception of the masses' achieved through 'spells concocted by morally unsettled and mentally confused intellectuals'. It thrives 'where men, and intellectuals above all, have lost their roots and solidity and have been pried loose from the social fabric of the family, the succession of generations, neighbourliness, and other true communities'.[76]

By neglecting such questions the hard-boiled economists have softened up understanding of the market for the market-socialist assault. But it cannot be repeated too often that a competitive market only makes sense in a particular spiritual, moral and political context. I have been calling this setting civil association. It might be called bourgeois civilisation. The name does not matter. The fundamental point is that market competition is not a technique that can be transplanted into a different system based on political power, as today's new socialists imagine.[77]

Conclusion

Allow me to return to the theme of the three inseparables. Central to my argument is the claim that particular beliefs about 'character', the 'role of government' and the type of 'unity' go together. Different combinations of the elements are possible but they may not be consistent. Certain New Right schools have only embraced part of what is necessary in a civil association. Some focused on limiting government—and there need to be strong limits on the tasks of the state—but it also has an important role in maintaining the conditions for liberty. The challenge today is to confine government to its proper tasks rather than to seek to reduce its scope as an end in itself. The central issue is not the size of government alone, but its character.

The great fear of *laissez-faire* economists who wish to see a minimal state is politicisation, that is the concentration of power in political hands. This is an entirely justified fear in the 20th century and no genuine enthusiast for freedom could avoid sharing this concern. But to resist the concentration of power is to advocate the dispersal of decision making to people assumed to be capable of bearing responsibility, respecting others, and making intelligent choices. It rests on a high view of human character, yet the rational utility calculators advance a low view of human motivation, based on maximising satisfactions. They should not allow their concern with prediction to obscure their understanding of the real complexity of human motivation. To do so means they have no real weapons against socialists who stress 'active citizenship' and service of the common good. The economist may point out that 'active citizen' means politically active and he would be right. And he may argue, as the public-choice school does, that claims to be benevolent may disguise naked self-interest, and he would be right. But care should be taken to offer a better alternative and not to fall into the trap of cynicism about all idealism.

In a corporate association people are perceived as having an assigned role. In a civil association they are expected to develop their character, to think and judge and to live their lives as a struggle to be better people. The commitment to individualism needs to be tempered by an awareness of the limits of our knowledge. Hayek distinguished between two rational traditions which emerged from the 18th century enlightenment: one he calls constructivist rationalism and the other, evolutionary rationalism. (Popper called them naïve rationalism and critical rationalism, respectively.) Naïve or constructivist rationalism over-estimates what man can accomplish, whereas critical or evolutionary rationalism is aware of human limitations. Its main message is that we cannot know the future and that, therefore, we should allow many people to try out their own ideas. This process has two advantages: first it means that we employ more talents in discovering the truth through trial and error, and second experiments are attempted on a scale which reduces the harm that results when they are based on mistakes.

According to Hayek our knowledge is inherited. Mind is the product of cultural evolution, based more on imitation than reason. Yet we are afflicted by a 'fatal conceit', namely the 'idea that the ability to acquire skills stems from reason'. Learning how to behave, he says, is the *source* of insight, not the *result* of it. What we call 'mind' is not like the brain, something we are born with, nor is it produced by the brain but something the brain helps us acquire as we grow up.[78] Hayek might have said, we *are* what we learn. We would be wise to remind ourselves from time to time of our dependence on others and on the civilisation we have been fortunate enough to inherit.

Hayek's aim was to blend the conservative concern of writers like Burke, who emphasised that tradition was a learnable body of knowledge and morals, with classical liberal attachment to change and self-conscious improvement. We should respect tradition and recognise that we cannot start again from scratch, says Hayek. And we should recognise that the minds that some intellectuals fancy to be capable of remodelling whole societies are themselves the products of tradition. But we are not locked in. We can improve our institutions, so long as we are modest. We can become born-again men, but we cannot devise a born-again culture.

Classical-liberals should also acknowledge that their philosophy rests on a sense of community, and one that deserves the name. But it is a sense of unity which brings us together in creating opportunity for all rather than one which combines us in pursuit of an end result. Many free marketeers have been reluctant to speak of community, because the term has been purloined by socialists who have political power on their minds. But talk of community need not be a prelude to coercive political action, it can also be justified pride in sharing responsibility for maintaining in good shape the institutions and personal virtues which give everyone a chance. To speak of our 'social nature' does not imply a 'political nature'. Quite the reverse.

And it rests on a view of human character which sees people, not as innately good, nor infinitely malleable through education, but which emphasises our mutual interdependence. It goes without saying that the coercive power of the state should not be employed to produce a particular character, but that supporters of liberty should in their private lives do their bit to maintain in being the institutions which bring out the best in people, above all the traditional family but also the voluntary associations for helping one another which historically were part of the fabric of life. The reason for reducing the scope of the welfare state, therefore, is not only that private organisations will provide better services, but also that it will restore the role of voluntary associations whose task is character building as well as service provision.

Thus, finally to sum up: the system of voluntary exchange developed historically in a particular moral setting—namely bourgeois culture, for want of a better term—and it can only be understood as part of this setting. The system of voluntary exchange at agreed prices can be lifted out of context and discussed as an abstraction, but any such discussion is only dealing with a part of the reality, not the whole. Because our eyes have been fixed on 'the economy' we have not been alert to mistaken doctrines which have caused family breakdown and turned voluntary associations—once sources of that strength of character which insulates nations from tyranny—directly or indirectly into instruments of the state.

3

The Three Inseparables and the Sources of Collectivism

HOW CAN we explain the continued appeal of collectivism? What are the elements that make up this complex of ideas and why does it retain its allure for so many people despite its manifest failure to produce the results expected by early enthusiasts?

The Rationales For Collectivism (Corporate Association)

How can we explain the continuing support for collectivism? Historically, five main grounds for corporate association have proved powerful: religion, production enhancement, majoritarian democracy, redistributive justice and social therapy.

The Religious Corporation

The medieval Catholic Church saw itself as the all-embracing educator and arbiter of truth. Today the ethos of the Catholic Church is compatible with a free society, but in medieval times it was not. It was a corporation devoted to the worship of God and the enjoyment of His grace, with the Pope as its head, supreme legislator and judge, enunciator of doctrine, and guardian of learning. His task was to impart Christian knowledge to each successive generation.[1] In the greater part of Europe during the tenth, eleventh, twelfth, and thirteenth centuries, said Adam Smith, the constitution of the church of Rome was:

> the most formidable combination that ever was formed against the authority and security of civil government, as well as against the liberty, reason, and happiness of mankind, which can flourish only where civil government is able to protect them. In that constitution the grossest delusions of superstition were supported in such a manner by the private interests of so great a number

> of people as put them out of all danger from any assault of human reason.[2]

The corporatism of the medieval Church of Rome appealed to many secular rulers, and by the fifteenth century the independent and sacred authority of the Church was being assumed by kings.[3] Some monarchs had control, not only of schools and universities, but also of intellectual and moral guidance. The Spanish Inquisition, for instance, had begun its work by the end of 15th century.

States linked with Calvinism extended such doctrines into the early modern age. In sixteenth century Geneva, for example, the members of the 'corporation' were recognised to be a mixture of the 'elect' (those predestined for salvation) and the 'reprobate'. The rulers were not themselves seen as agents of salvation, but their task, according to Oakeshott:

> was to organise and direct a substantive condition of human circumstance in which the conduct of each of their subjects conformed at all times to the purpose of the enterprise: the glorification of God whose wrath would be visited upon a delinquent community. This single purpose to which all activities whatsoever were to be assimilated, was set out in instrumental rules, regulations, directives, and commands which appropriately, recognised no distinction between 'public' and 'private' and allowed no divergence from the uniform purity of appearance.[4]

Such doctrines form part of the parentage of twentieth century totalitarianism.

Production Enhancement

The purposes of the state in medieval and early modern times were typically associated with religion, but Francis Bacon, in *New Atlantis* (published in 1627, the year after his death) developed a theory of the state as 'an economy' or development corporation. According to Bacon, the purpose of life was not preparation for the life to come, but to develop the Earth's resources. His materialism, however, retained a religious inspiration: material progress was to be for the glory of God, not man.[5]

Later enthusiasts for the same doctrine, including the early utopian socialists such as St Simon, offered a version without religious faith. People were owners, managers, workers and no more, and the purpose of the state as 'an economy' was to produce, redistribute, and to satisfy human wants.[6] Brotherly love played its part in the earlier utopian schemes, though by the end of the nineteenth century it was barely visible in the more technocratic versions of socialism which came to dominate. Sidney Webb, for example, described his view of man as follows:

> The perfect and fitting development of each individual is not necessarily the utmost and highest cultivation of his own personality, but the filling, in the best possible way, of his humble function in the great social machine.[7]

This view has come under effective criticism from Hayek for its failure to be aware of the limits of human knowledge. The character and fallibility of our knowledge means that detailed central direction of economic and social life is unworkable and must always produce unexpected results. Knowledge is dispersed, and so our institutions must be decentralised.

There are, however, elements of this doctrine in the new socialism of Tony Blair. The nation is to be managed as 'an economy': it does not *have* an economy it *is* an economy. Production is to be enhanced through a government investment bank and there is to be 'partnership' between government and industry. Partnership, along with 'stakeholder', are the new code words for the corporate state, a doctrine described as clearly by Samuel Brittan as anyone:

> In essence it amounts to the belief in informal directorship of our affairs by the men who run large organisations. 'Gt. Britain Ltd' is not a bad caricature and conveys the flavour of people who really know what makes things tick, sorting things out together 'without any ideological nonsense'.

He continues:

> It is all too easy to imagine an *ersatz* populism under which a supposedly left-wing government would try to make the world

> safe for high technology 'Big Business', in which 'Britain must be in the lead'. The representatives of the technostructure might be more than happy to accept the charade of government-appointed directors, or even of worker representatives—and have the Minister of Technology to breakfast—in return for a real insulation from market disciplines and the negative control of the Treasury.[8]

According to this view, the task of the state is to manage the economy. The market is understood as a mere technique to be harnessed and is valued because it generates more goods, not because it is the system most consistent with human dignity and most based on mutual respect. The dangers inherent in tearing the market economy from its moral setting have been considered in Chapter 2.

Majoritarian Democracy

One of the more perverse developments during the 20th century has been the corruption of parliament. At one time it was a critic of the ruler and a partner in maintaining the law of the land. Gradually there have been three main changes. First, it has become a place where private interests bargain with governments for benefits. Second, it has become more like a meeting of shareholders in a corporate enterprise. National targets are set for this or that and proposals put to the vote, with the outcome rarely in doubt. And thirdly, the laws it makes have increasingly became mere management instructions.

Hayek regarded the tendency for the same authority that makes the rules of justice also to direct the day-to-day affairs of government to be the root of the problem.[9] The doctrine of the rule of law in its narrowest sense of requiring mere lawfulness is inadequate: what is crucial is the type of law, namely whether it is 'moral' or 'instrumental'.[10] In the 20th century, to defend more or less any action taken by a political majority, it is enough to insist on its democratic credentials, which means that the victorious party wishing to pursue a harmful or unpopular policy need only point for justification to some words it put in its manifesto. In this manner, unlimited power has crept in by the back door.

Throughout British history Parliament's task was to protect the people from the abuse of kingly power. Sixteenth century speculation focused on the origin of kingly authority, stressing in some cases the social contract and the right of citizens to depose tyrants. And there was an established tradition of deposing tyrannical kings, such as Edward II.

The natural law theorists of the seventeenth century also provided a rationale for limiting the powers of kings. There were natural or higher laws, they said, and these fundamental laws set limits to the exercise of power. Federal theories stressed the separation of powers. Others emphasised rights to be informed, to petition, remonstrate, and approve but without challenging sovereign authority. Parliamentary democracy itself provided for periodic elections and debate in public. All in their own way were alternative methods of limiting the abuse of power, but later thinkers forgot the importance of such limitations.

By the Second World War, understanding of earlier theories of parliament's role had been almost forgotten. Democracy had come to mean the unlimited power of parliament, that is, the majority in parliament (which has invariably been a minority in the country). Few despots of old ever succeeded in making a reality of the divine right of kings, and would have looked with envy on the success of devotees of the divine right of parliament.

One of the notions employed to extend unlimited arbitrary political power has been the argument that market forces should be replaced by 'democracy', which more accurately reflects people's views. This amounts, in reality, to saying that 'market forces' should be replaced by 'political forces' but such critics do not see the qualitative difference between the two. Market principles describe a *process* in which people are free to pursue their own version of the good life. In the social order desired by socialists most spheres are to be politicised, with the result that the government will predominate in dictating how we should live. Rival visions will be suppressed or crowded out. Nor do socialists seem conscious that the poorest people are at a disadvantage in a highly politicised system. In a free society those poor people who hope for a better life can fulfil their aspirations by making a personal choice to work hard and save. A politicised society requires the ambitious poor to organise politically to fulfil their hopes.

Socialists frequently claim to be concerned about economic concentration, which, they believe, has implications for political power. Money can buy political power, they say. But their remedy is concentrated political power. Reverting again to the 'three inseparables', reminds us of the importance of being suspicious of all concentrations of power, private or public. Competition and the maximum room for individual initiative encourage the wide dispersal of economic power. Egalitarians display no awareness that power concentrated in political hands is a far more menacing threat than power in private hands. Imagine that one of the leading electronics manufacturers somehow established an absolute monopoly. It would have massive income at its disposal, but the worst thing any such company could do would be to push up the price of CD players or perhaps make bad quality products. In a competitive market competitors would soon replace any such monopolist. But consider the worst action a government could take: it has the police, prisons, tax collectors and officials, not to mention the army, enabling it to kill, torture, imprison, confiscate possessions and disregard individual rights.

The egalitarian might retort that a monopolistic company might have so much money it could buy political power. This may be so but then the threat would be from the abuse of *political* power not economic power. The fundamental problem remains how to avoid the abuse of state power. The remedy is to put severe limits on the uses of political power so that no amount of economic power can buy unlimited political power. And, no less important, competition should be enforced to discourage concentrations of economic power and promote wide dispersal of resources. It does not matter how many cars or CD players or anything else a company sells, the money it accumulates does not become a threat until it is transformed into political power. The power to direct the police, the army and the prisons, and the capacity to levy taxes and manage people's lives are the chief threats to individual liberty and, therefore, the primary abuses to be avoided.

The argument that a system of democratic accountability is more representative than 'market forces' has a strong appeal to some, but it is based on three fundamental errors.

First, it assumes a political decision-making process, which inevitably means that the majority view (actually the ruling view whether it is a majority or not) will prevail over the minority (non-ruling) opinion. A market system, however, allows choice and initiative. It can be likened to a 'daily referendum', as my colleagues Ralph Harris and Arthur Seldon argued forcefully over many years.[11] Politicising choice may widen the opportunities open to those who benefit from the policies of the ruling party, but it suppresses the individual preferences of those who differ from the rulers of the day. Politically imposed choice always involves the imposed transfer of money from one set of voters to another. The higher ideal is to confine the political process to preserving the conditions for freedom and to prevent it becoming a weapon in the hands of any victorious faction.

Second, the political process has shown itself to be vulnerable to concentrated special interests. As Mancur Olson has demonstrated, lobbyists representing narrow concentrated interests are better able to exert influence than voices representing the common good.[12] The main reason is that politicians react to the people who bring themselves to their attention. Special interests have a lot to gain from hiring lobbyists and conducting publicity campaigns. The common good, or the interest of the vast majority of consumers or voters, can easily be forgotten as politicians try to be responsive to the people with whom they are in face to face contact. Economists have called this process 'rent seeking', that is the seeking through political manipulation of a return over and above the income available in a competitive market. Arthur Seldon calls it 'the privileges extracted from the political process without serving the tax-paying public'.[13]

Third, those who demand that 'democracy' should replace market forces tend to assume a social system divided between the relatively poor majority and the rich minority. They intend that the majority of voters should use their political power to confiscate the ill-gotten gains of the rich. But as Friedman points out, there is more than one possible voting coalition. Yes, the poor majority may combine against the rich. But equally, the middle class may combine against both the poor and the rich. Such a voting combination is so common, says Milton Friedman, that it has the status of a law, which he calls Director's Law: 'Public expenditures are made for the primary benefit of the middle class, and financed with taxes which are borne in considerable part by the poor and rich.'[14]

Several socialist writers have also drawn attention to middle-class capture. Julian Le Grand's *The Strategy of Equality* concludes: 'Almost all public expenditure on the social services in Britain benefits the better off to a greater extent than the poor.' Equality, in any sense of the term, has not been achieved. In all relevant areas 'there persist substantial inequalities in public expenditure, in use, in opportunity, in access and in outcomes'.[15] The problem is not confined to Britain. David Thomson has shown how one generation of New Zealanders, those currently retired, secured for itself advantages at the expense of the general population.[16]

For these reasons, replacing market forces with political forces will not have the claimed effects, not least because voters will change their expectations once it is recognised that the political process is a scramble for benefits. At least two reactions are possible. One is to get organised to make sure your side wins. This reaction has been the norm during the twentieth century. The other is to confine the political system to making the rules which serve all equally and forbid the law from being used to secure advantages for one class over another (see below, p. 114). This is the urgent and neglected task of the day.

The term democracy has come to be used in a very loose manner in modern times. The central issue is not whether we are governed by 'the few' or 'the many'. Of fundamental importance is the *method* of rule: specifically, is government open or closed?

A dictatorship may allow its people a wide latitude, and a democracy may narrow the scope for private initiative in favour of political decisions. Moreover, the majority in a democracy may discriminate against the minority. It is possible, therefore, for a system of 'rule by the few' to conduct affairs in an open, democratic spirit and for majority rule to function in a closed, secretive manner. Some thinkers on the left now recognise the dangers of excessive secrecy and elective dictatorship.[17]

The ideal is a democratic system based on a universal franchise, giving us the right to get rid of governments in regular and free elections, combined with an open method of ruling. The spirit of democracy requires an open style, not merely the outward forms of democracy. Modern democracy has come to mean little more than a requirement that élite bands of rivals submit themselves to election periodically. The election does little more than legitimise their unlimited power for a fixed period. But a government should also rely on what late medieval and early modern writers called 'counsel and consent'. That is, there would be wide awareness of issues under discussion, wide availability of information, and free discussion.

Victimism and the Therapeutic State

Let me now turn to a final doctrine justifying collectivism, namely victimism.

During the nineteenth century a view of the state charged with the duties of a therapist developed. It was to cure diseases such as poverty, insecurity, the feeling of being unimportant, industrial society and 'alienation'. According to Oakeshott:

> Here, a state is understood to be an association of invalids, all victims of the same disease and incorporated in seeking relief from their common ailment; and the office of government is a remedial engagement. Rulers are ... the directors of a sanatorium from which no patient may discharge himself by a choice of his own.[18]

During the eighteenth century the closely-related doctrine of the state organised for secular schooling developed as an alternative to states inspired by religion. The enlightened despots of the 18th century pursued the common good guided by reason rather than revelation, unlike Calvinists, medieval Catholics and Puritans. Prussia under Frederick the Great (king from 1740-1786) was at the forefront of these developments and education in Prussia during the 18th and 19th centuries was intended to make individuals more useful to the state, that is, to discharge their allotted tasks.[19]

This doctrine of the therapeutic state had an appeal to people who lacked confidence in their potential to take advantage of freedom. Historically, there have always been people who have not welcomed liberty, but seen it as a burden. The dissolution of the old certainties of belief, occupation, and status was welcomed by those who had some confidence in their ability to cope and prosper, but there were many who felt no such optimism. The counterpart of the commercial adventurer or the artisan confident of his skill was the displaced labourer; and the counterpart of the inner-directed man was the dispossessed believer.[20]

Political movements developed to exploit the fears of the insecure, usually led by men with scant respect for their followers. These new leaders, said Oakeshott, were:

> persons who have themselves just enough individuality to derive some satisfaction from the adventure of making choices but too little to seek it anywhere save in commanding others, persons who can appear as both the image and the master of their followers, whose concern is to exercise power, and who are naturally indisposed to put a term to their activities by urging their followers to cultivate self-reliance or even to be critical of their impulses.[21]

Typically the followers had 'rights' which the leaders would supply. Marxism exploited these sentiments most fully by presenting liberty as the creed of the already privileged, a class doctrine. Socialism would restore power to its rightful owners, the masses. But as the Russian masses were to learn, their leaders saw them as role-playing followers, devoid of moral qualities, ready for moulding into 'new men' or to be imprisoned or killed if they wilfully resisted.

The notion of the therapeutic state is closely linked to the modern idea of the victim, whose situation needs to be put right by the state-as-therapist. Victim status today is much sought after. The American political scientist Aaron Wildavsky has calculated that 374 per cent of Americans define themselves as victims![22] At least six advantages can be identified: it justifies anger or hatred; it provides a rationale for compensation; it justifies political privileges (positive discrimination); it excuses bad behaviour by the victim; it relieves the victim of personal responsibility; and it puts critics on the defensive. The importance of victim status was revealed in the controversy involving American Supreme Court nominee, Clarence Thomas, and Anita Hill. Both presented themselves as victims, one a woman the other a black, and these appeals dominated discussion rather than reason or truth.

Victim status is politically valuable because there have been *real* victims. American blacks, in particular, were badly treated historically. However, there is more than one possible reaction to mistreatment, and not all such reactions are consistent with a free society. For instance, to sympathise with a victim does not require support for violence. Yet this was the trap sprung by late-1960s campaigners for black power. You are either for us or against us, they said.

The early civil rights movement, under the leadership of Martin Luther King was very different. King's philosophy was a cross between Old Testament righteousness, New Testament forgiveness and the theories of non-violent protest championed by Gandhi. He was much influenced by the theology of Reinhold Niebuhr, who warned against campaigns based on righteous indignation. Resentment, he said, was 'merely the egoistic side of the sense of injustice.' The campaigner should always acknowledge the common humanity of both victim and oppressor.[23] As Niebuhr wrote in *Moral Man and Immoral Society*:

> The discovery of elements of common human frailty in the foe and, concomitantly, the appreciation of all human life as possessing transcendent worth, creates attitudes which transcend social conflict and thus mitigate its cruelties. It binds human beings together by reminding them of the common roots and similar character of both their vices and their virtues. These attitudes of repentance which recognise that the evil in the foe is also in the self, and these impulses of love which claim kinship with all men in spite of social conflict are the peculiar gifts of religion to the human spirit.[24]

King resisted campaigners who wanted to present their struggle as one between black and white. While I will fight the white man, 'to get out from under his subjugation', said King, 'I will also try to understand him and I will not try to defeat him'.[25]

This Gandhian spirit is captured in King's famous 'I Have a Dream' speech, delivered in August 1963 in Washington, DC:

> I have a dream that my four little children will one day live in a nation where they will not be judged by the color of their skin but by the content of their character. I have a dream today!
>
> I have a dream that one day, down in Alabama, with its vicious racists, with its governor having his lips dripping with the words of interposition and nullification, one day, right there in Alabama, little black boys and black girls will be able to join hands with little white boys and white girls as sisters and brothers. I have a dream today![26]

By the late 1960s, however, the idea that the civil rights movement should be built on Christian love and forgiveness was being treated with derision. Instead of equality of opportunity, the new generation of leaders demanded 'reparations'. King had stressed hard work, strong families, and religious faith. 'Nothing,' King argued, 'is so much needed as a secure family life for a people to pull themselves out of poverty'. The new generation of leaders denounced such values as the ideology of whites, embraced only by black Uncle Toms. Ironically, some of the main enthusiasts for aggression were the movement's white supporters, whilst the majority of blacks supported King. Charles Sykes in his insightful study, *A Nation of Victims*, quotes a 1966 survey which found that King received the approval of 88 per cent of black Americans whereas black-power advocate Stokely Carmichael won the approval of only 19 per cent.[27]

Some activists drew on the extremist writing of the arch-exponent of revolutionary violence, Frantz Fanon. Writing about French colonialism, Fanon urged victims of oppression to be ready for violence at all times. He rejected any notion of a shared moral order because it created 'an atmosphere of submission and inhibition' among colonised peoples. The victim of oppression 'laughs in mockery when Western values are mentioned in front of him.' They 'insult them, and vomit them up'.[28]

One of the targets of the militant campaigners was a paper called *The Negro Family: The Case For National Action*, written in 1965 by Daniel Moynihan, then a White House aide. He argued that the black community was being destroyed by the breakdown of the family, measured in rising illegitimacy and desertions by fathers:

> At the heart of the deterioration of the fabric of Negro society is the deterioration of the Negro family. It is the fundamental source of weakness of the Negro community at the present time ... Unless this damage is repaired, all the effort to end discrimination and poverty and injustice will come to little.[29]

Moynihan's statement was bitterly denounced, with white academics in the forefront, including William Ryan, whose book *Blaming the Victim*,[30] first published in 1971, supplied the catch-phrase still in common use. The new 'blame the victim' ideology, Ryan accepted, was very different from the old racism. Its adherents included sympathetic social scientists with a genuine commitment to reform, but they had been duped. Old racists believed that blacks were defective because they were 'born that way', but the emphasis on character and personal responsibility was not an improvement because it still located the explanation within the victim rather than in 'the system'.

Ryan's approach is exemplified by his attack on the Coleman Report (*Equality of Educational Opportunity*), a major study carried out by sociologist James Coleman and published by the US Office of Education in 1966. It was, said Ryan, 'an impeccably liberal and scientific work'. Coleman reported that black parents were found to be highly interested in the educational success of their children, but that 'this interest often does not get translated into action which supports the child's work in school.'[31] And the data, Coleman found, give a picture of students also reporting high interest in success which 'was not translated through effective action into achievement'. Is this or is this not, asked Ryan rhetorically, 'a clear case of blaming the victim?'[32] In his view, to draw attention to personal responsibility at all was inescapably to apportion blame and on that account wrong.

Ryan's approach to family breakdown and illegitimacy was similar. In a chapter entitled 'The Prevalence of Bastards', he dismissed personal choice, character, or the moral climate of the community as having any relevance. 'The "problem" of illegitimacy is not due to promiscuity, immorality, or culturally-based variations in sexual habits; it is due to discrimination and gross inequities between rich and poor, and more particularly between white and black.' It reflected the 'intent of the dominant majority to keep the poor in their place'.[33]

He rejected the argument of some white social scientists that black family breakdown was the 'heritage of slavery' because some slave owners had not allowed man and wife to live together. This argument, said Ryan, is an ingenious cop out:

> As the murderer pleads guilty to manslaughter to avoid a conviction that might lead to his being electrocuted, liberal America today is pleading guilty to savagery and oppression against the Negro of one hundred years ago in order to escape trial for the crimes of today.[34]

He was no less uncompromising in his explanation of black criminality. The victim-blaming theory of crime comprises four propositions. First, 'Crime is dramatically more prevalent in the slums and among the poor'; second, 'the criminality of the poor is a result of social conditions which, in effect, warp their character and behaviour'; third, 'these lower-class criminals make up a distinct sub-group in the population; and fourth, the purpose of police activity is to suppress them. These formulations, he says, are 'extremely plausible', but in fact are 'the most outrageous collection of non-facts imaginable'. If the theory seemed to be supported by the presence of more blacks in jail, this was because they were arrested more frequently, whereas whites were 'usually left alone' by the racist police.[35]

Thus, for Ryan and similar academics, to assign any responsibility to a person was *blaming* the victim. All human conduct should be explained as the outcome of outside forces—the system. The public policy conclusion was that political power should be used to modify the 'outside forces'. Ryan's argument is compelling because it appeals to our sympathy. Many blacks were mistreated. No reasonable person could fail to condemn lynchings and the systematic denial of civil rights in the Deep South. But as inspirational leaders like Gandhi and Martin Luther King showed, it is how the victim reacts that matters most. They should not be quiescent; they should resist injustice, but in a manner compatible with a mutually respecting moral community. They should not replace the white man's hate with their own, but build a better world for all and they should not react with hatred or retaliation, but in order to maintain the values which allow diverse peoples to live together in peace. Martin Luther King's views were based on moral principles which could serve as a basis for freedom. He appealed to the best in people. Ryan's appeal is to the most base of human instincts.

Indeed, Ryan considers personal responsibility to be of no relevance. He cites an activist friend of his who tried everything to generate citizen support for the welfare rights movement, including 'heartbreaking stories of life on welfare'. To Ryan's disgust, most of his listeners seemed 'unable to rid themselves of the ingrained belief that getting money without working for it—no matter how worthy and touching the recipient may be—is illicit, slothful and vaguely criminal.'[36] In Ryan's world-view, there was no place for such acts of conscience.

Yet, in reality the 'victim' may have contributed to his own predicament. If the remedy does, in practice, lie within the control of the victim then any observer should be free to say so. Traditionally American blacks reacted to their predicament by hard work, good character, thrift, self-sacrifice and family loyalty. As a strategy it worked, as the millions of American blacks who made it to the middle-class can testify, and as many black writers including Thomas Sowell and Walter Williams have convincingly argued. It also worked for the Jews and many other ethnic groups in America.

As Charles Sykes notes in *A Nation of Victims*, the main message of victim status is: '*I am not at fault. [Fill in the Blank] made me do it*.'[37] But this undermining of responsibility has been fatally damaging for poor groups. They cannot afford delusions

Another reason for the appeal of victimism in the 1960s and 1970s was the animosity to guilt. There were many who hoped for a blame-free, guilt-free society. But the release from responsibility is applied only to the self-defined victim, not to others. There is always someone *else* to blame.[38] Not only does it relieve the self-defined victim of responsibility, it justifies rage towards oppressors. Worse still it justifies rage towards groups. All whites can justly be hated, whether the particular individual is right or wrong. It is very far from absolving everyone of blame. On the contrary, victimism heightens the atmosphere of blame, whilst absolving victims of responsibility.

Victim status is closely allied with the medicalisation of conditions. Conditions like stress have become conditions that can only be overcome with expert therapy or counselling. But they are further examples of the flight from personal responsibility. The latest such cry is post-traumatic stress syndrome, otherwise known as being upset after a serious incident like an accident. This condition can only be resolved with help from highly trained counsellors, though the victim is afforded much relief by the award of compensatory damages.

The result of this attitude is that genuine victims become less able to handle pain or loss. Instead of coping, they say to themselves, it *should* not have happened. And instead of digging deep within for strength, or sharing their problem with a friend or relative, the victim asks, 'Who is to blame and who should compensate me?' No one, it seems, should ever have to sacrifice anything, or struggle against adversity.

It is also accompanied by hyper-sensitivity in the use of language. It would be wrong to call a black person a 'nigger' or to address him as 'boy'. From this reasonable base we are led to the ludicrous ban in some circles on the use of the term 'Dutch treat', because it is insulting to the Dutch. As Sykes remarks, 'Sensitivity' transforms the aggrieved self into 'the imperial arbiter of behaviour'. Everyone must now accommodate himself to the feelings of the victim.[39]

A further consequence is that reason is undermined. The non-victim is defined as incapable of understanding the plight of the victim: no white can understand the predicament of the black; no man can comprehend the predicament of a woman. Any comment the outsider makes is unavoidably prejudiced and so the possibility of resolving conflicts by the exchange of views is ruled out. All that is needed is to make a charge of racism or sexism and it is game, set and match to the victim.[40]

The sensitivity that requires others to adjust to the self-defined sense of grievance of the victim is sharply in contrast with the morality of freedom Kant had in mind when he formulated the 'categorical imperative'. And it is not consistent with the 'golden rule'—do unto others as you would have them do unto you—which also enjoins us to take the feelings of others into account. For centuries, moral systems have urged us to try to see ourselves as others see us; to sympathise with the feelings of other people; and not to exempt ourselves from observing rules which apply to everyone else. But victim status justifies a quite different ethos. Only the victim can judge. This makes the sensitivity required very different from the ordinary civility expected in a typical daily exchange. Victim status is the perfect excuse for self-exemption from rules which rightly apply to others. It is quite incompatible with the mutual respect of free and responsible persons.

Victimism also undermines real human decency, while pretending to appeal to it. The victim is different from the person in need of help. A victim resents help; instead he demands *rights*. Traditionally helping another was regarded as a duty or obligation embodying mutual respect. It might be a duty undertaken as a burden, or as a joy, but however the duty was perceived, there was a kind of equality between giver and receiver, with the giver offering assistance on the assumption that the help was temporary. He was tiding the receiver over until he got back on his feet. The receiver accepted help on the same terms, and resolved to pay back the help, if not necessarily pound for pound, then by returning the favour in a manner open to him on some future occasion. This mutual respect is captured in the story of Stephen Blackpool in Dickens' *Hard Times* (below, p. 126). But the new doctrine of the victim accepts no mutuality in the relationship. The victim demands one-sided rights.

Although victim status brings political power, it is a trap. It robs the victim of personal responsibility, the only real source of self respect. This lingering feeling that respect has been diminished may explain the stridency of the demand for rights. Assistance must be as of right because a right suggests respect. But the rights demanded by victims are not like other universal rights. They are special rights given only to victims.

Consider the disabled, one of the more recent groups to discover the political pull that victim status brings. Take the example of a wheelchair-bound accident victim in his thirties injured at the height of his powers. Imagine that he takes up sport and overcomes obstacles to win a competition. His is a triumph of spirit over adversity. He is not only respected, but admired. Because he has shown by his actions that he is doing his bit, he can receive help honourably. And the giver can assist without fear of seeming to patronise. There is mutual respect.

Compare him with the wheelchair bound person who lies flat on his back blocking traffic in Parliament Square to demand the enactment of a new law against 'discrimination'. He demands that no employer should take disability into account when recruiting employees. But such a right does not bring real respect. The disabled person may have a job by right, but he will not be able to do it without help. Yet no one at work will be able to admit that he is helping. The disabled person will have to live a lie.

There will be no triumph of spirit and no courage. There will still be help, but it will be hidden by the coercion. It will be whispered help. And there will be no reciprocity or mutual respect in the relationship because it is based on force.

There are universal rights and there are victim's rights. They are not the same. Instead, the disabled ought to appeal, not to force, but to the best in people. Yes, they should appeal to sympathy. No, helping another person out of sympathy need not be patronising, but given in the knowledge that anyone can end up in a wheelchair—in the spirit of 'there but for the grace of God go I'. If disabled people find that help is given in a patronising manner, let them campaign, not for rights, but for the help to be given in the right spirit of mutual respect.

Finally, one of the least edifying aspects of victimism is the manner in which victimist ideology is promoted by groups who base their claim on the grievances of others. For instance, middle-class blacks based their claim for positive discrimination on the genuine injustices done to other blacks in the past. The result is that middle class blacks get privileges such as promotions in the workplace which they do not deserve. Middle class feminist women often make similar demands. They claim that women in the past have been discriminated against, and insist upon job promotions today, when they have personally suffered no loss and may not deserve on merit the job appointment they crave.

Redistributive Justice[41]

One of the most damaging doctrines of the modern age is social justice. At first glance, it seems to be something any reasonable person might want, like 'fair play' or 'fairness'. Most importantly, social justice is deliberately confused with the relief of poverty. But social justice is a doctrine which calls for political power to be used to make people materially more equal, and as such, is incompatible with a free society. Fairness and justice are good things; the abuse of political power under the guise of creating social justice is not.

I will comment on ten of the main rationales for the pursuit of social justice, concentrating on the most influential.

1. The Duty to Relieve Poverty

There has long been a widely-supported belief that we all have a duty to prevent starvation and in Britain from medieval times until the twentieth century this obligation was placed upon local public authorities (see below p. 134). The problem today is that the wide support for the relief of hardship has been exploited by egalitarians to cultivate support for equality, a doctrine calling for the power of the state to be used, not to assist the poor, but to equalise people.

Advocates of equalisation, have consequently been able to exploit support for the relief of poverty by falsely characterising measures designed to equalise people as measures to relieve suffering.

A major landmark was the 'rediscovery' of poverty in the 1960s. Instead of defining poverty in terms of hardship, the poverty line was calculated in relation to average earnings. Early studies by investigators like Rowntree used an absolute standard. He defined 'primary poverty' as, falling below earnings sufficient to 'obtain the minimum necessaries for the maintenance of merely physical efficiency'.[42] The chief difficulty for poverty campaigners in the 1960s was that, on such a definition, no one in Britain was poor. The focus, therefore, switched to relative poverty.

Although the distinction has come to be discussed as one between absolute and relative poverty, this mis-states the difference, because any definition of poverty must be relative to the extent that public conceptions of hardship change over time. But the fact that conceptions of hardship have changed as prosperity has increased does not justify linking the poverty line to average or median earnings. This device has the result of defining a large proportion of the population as always poor, without regard to the actual standard of life enjoyed.

The Joseph Rowntree Foundation Inquiry into Income and Wealth of 1995 received considerable attention for its claim that: 'income inequality in the UK grew rapidly between 1977 and 1990, reaching a higher level than recorded since the War'.[43] It went on to say that, 'Over the period 1979 to 1992 the poorest 20-30 per cent of the population failed to benefit from economic growth, in contrast to the rest of the post-war period'.[44]

The Rowntree Inquiry figures rely mostly on the government's *Households Below Average Income* series, excluding the self-employed whose income declarations are believed to be unreliable.[45] The Inquiry repeated the finding of the 1994 HBAI report that total average income grew by 36 per cent between 1977 and 1990, while the average income of the poorest tenth remained the same in 1991-92 as in 1979 before deducting housing costs, and was 9 per cent lower after deducting housing costs. The press release reveals the political intentions of the committee of inquiry. It said:

> The Inquiry warns that market forces, left to themselves, cannot deliver the investment that will most benefit the economy and society as a whole. It concludes that a range of co-ordinated initiatives is required to address the many causes of growing inequality.[46]

The Rowntree Inquiry has not been alone in exaggerating the extent of poverty. The Child Poverty Action Groups is among the worst culprits. The official *Low Income Families* series was published from 1972-1985 and defined poverty as 'on or below' the then supplementary benefit level. At that time CPAG authors tended to define poverty as the supplementary benefit level plus 40 per cent.[47] More recently the CPAG has preferred to draw the line at a different point. The *Low Income Families* series was superseded by *Households Below Average Income,* which covered those below 50 per cent of average income, the definition of poverty preferred by the European Commission. The Child Poverty Action Group typically uses this figure to make claims about the number of children in poverty each year.[48] For example the CPAG claimed in June 1995 that 4.3m children lived in poverty compared with 1.4m in 1979.[49] Its publications have regularly exaggerated poverty. For example a 1994 publication, *Family Fortunes,* describes Britain as:

> a society in which 4.1 million children, 32 per cent of the total, live in poverty; in which the poorest 10 per cent of families with children had an average household income £438 per annum lower in real terms in 1992 than in 1979, a period in which the disposable annual income of the richest 10 per cent rose by £13,900.[50]

The Low Pay Unit prefers 'two-thirds of median male earnings' as its definition of low pay. Not to be outdone, the Council of Europe goes further still and define its 'decency threshold' as £221.50 per week or £5.88 per hour in 1994. Data from the UK *New Earnings Survey 1994* showed that on this measure 37.3 per cent of workers earned less than the 'decency threshold'.[51]

The assertions of the Rowntree Inquiry and kindred organisations are contradicted by an independent study conducted by the Institute for Fiscal Studies (IFS) comparing household income and expenditure. The *Households Below Average Income* (HBAI) series relies on the *Family Expenditure Survey,* an annual sample survey based on about 7,000 households. Also using data from the *Family Expenditure Survey,* the IFS found marked differences between the expenditure and the income of households. The comparison shows that the gap between richer and poorer in terms of both income and expenditure did widen, as the Rowntree Inquiry claimed.[52] However, the IFS compared the expenditure of the bottom decile (by taking the 5th percentile) and the top decile (by taking the 95th percentile). The *income* of the 5th percentile stagnated between 1979 and 1992 before housing costs are deducted and fell by 18 per cent after housing costs are deducted. But the *expenditure* of the same percentile grew by 17 per cent before deduction of housing costs and by 14 per cent after deduction. Thus, say the IFS authors, 'the often quoted result that "the poor got poorer" over the 1980s is not upheld if expenditure is chosen as the measure of living standards'.[53]

The IFS report also allows a comparison with the Rowntree Inquiry claim that the bottom 20-30 per cent had not shared in the rising prosperity of the 1980s. The IFS found that the bottom 10 per cent (according to income) in 1992 spent on average 27 per cent more before deduction of housing costs than in 1979 (or 30 per cent more after deduction of housing costs), a finding it describes as 'startling'.[54] Even if the self-employed are taken out (as the Rowntree Inquiry did) the increase was about 24 per cent whether or not housing costs are included.[55] The second and third decile groups also increased their expenditure, but not by so much. The second decile group (according to income) increased spending by about 15 per cent and the third by about 8 per cent.[56]

The IFS examined the possibility that the difference was the result of increased debt, but found it not to be the reason.[57] The increase in self-employment explains some of the difference, but excluding the self-employed from the calculations still leaves an average increase in spending of 24 per cent.[58] Part of the remaining difference is explained by the increase in the number of people reporting zero or negative income. In 1979 26 individuals in the Family Expenditure Survey reported zero or negative incomes after deducting housing costs, whereas in 1992 133 did so. In many years, the average expenditure of those reporting no income exceeded the average for the whole population, because individuals resorted to their savings.[59]

However, the chief explanation given is that the households in the bottom decile according to income vary considerably from year to year and that, in any one year, the households in the bottom tenth may have savings on which they can draw. The IFS found that over the period 1979-1992, the proportion of pensioners in the bottom income decile fell, as they were replaced by working-age families. Some people, who are unemployed for a relatively short time, for instance, draw on their savings, whereas pensioners on average spend less than non-pensioners because they are more inclined to save from their income than to spend their savings.[60] This explains why the average increases in the expenditure of the second income decile (15 per cent before deduction of housing costs) and third income decile (8 per cent) (both of which included an increasing proportion of pensioners over the period) were lower than that the bottom income decile (27 per cent).[61]

Thus, in flat contradiction of the Joseph Rowntree Inquiry, the bottom 20-30 ranked by income spent in real terms considerably more in 1992 than in 1979 and thus shared in the increased prosperity of the period.[62]

A table in the 1995 edition of *Households Below Average Income* shows just how much variation there is between income and expenditure. Three per cent of those in the bottom decile according to income were in the highest decile for expenditure and 20 per cent were in the top 50 per cent. Only 33 per cent of the lowest decile according to income were in the lowest decile according to expenditure.[63] This variation shows the folly of building public policies on statistical evidence about aggregates. As I will argue in Chapter 6, it would be more effective to adopt a more personal approach which allows for human diversity.

But quite apart from the actual evidence of income and expenditure, it is important to distinguish between the relief of hardship and equalisation, because the former is consistent with limited government whilst the latter provides a rationale for unlimited arbitrary power. Is it plausible to uphold an absolute definition of poverty, when what constitutes hardship will inevitably change with general prosperity? In practice, the absolute standard will be a 'moving absolute'. The minimum standard of living could be defined at a particular time in terms of a basket of goods which can change over time as the consensus on the accepted minimum changes. To avoid constant political pressure for change or adjustment, the basket of goods might be fixed for a 5 or 10 year period. The poverty line thus defined would not be a permanent standard fixed for all time, but it would serve to limit the scope of political power. Alternative measures based on the constantly-changing average wage or the vague ambition to 'compress' income differentials allow wide scope for state coercion and put individual lives too much under the control of the authorities.

Again, if we recall the three inseparables, the assumptions of egalitarians become clearer. They do not see people as characters exercising intelligence, but individuals whose lives require management by the authorities. The confusion of poverty with inequality is part of a deliberate campaign to create a constituency for confiscatory political action, or what the Rowntree Inquiry prefers to call 'a range of co-ordinated initiatives'.

2. *Rewards According to Merit*

It is sometimes argued that all rewards should be deserved and frequently argued that some (high) incomes are not deserved. Such discussions are part and parcel of the human condition, and my only concern here is with this argument when it becomes a rationale for government action to assess how much a person is worth.

First of all, no one has enough knowledge to make any such political assessment. Considerable knowledge of past and present effort expended would be necessary to make a reasoned judgement, quite apart from knowledge of how effective and successful an individual employee was. In view of these complexities, it is very difficult to see how there could ever be an informed consensus on merit sufficient to justify political action.

There is a second consideration. Would we really want all rewards to depend on merit? Life would almost certainly be harder to bear if all rewards were thought to be deserved. At present we do not know why someone has a low income. It may be all they are capable of earning, or it may be that they consider a lower paid job more worthwhile, or perhaps the journey to work is more convenient. People do not necessarily maximise their incomes, and they may have good reasons for not doing so.

Third, a political mechanism rewarding people 'on merit' would undermine the incentive and signalling mechanisms which stimulate economic improvement. Individuals should be free to reap the reward of their own efforts. Income, like other prices, has a signalling function. It is not an overall assessment of our worth, but it does tell us how much our services are valued by an employer. A person dissatisfied with this evaluation is free to alter the skills he offers by retraining or to move to another place, where his services may be better appreciated. Moreover, the capacity of an organisation to pay higher incomes will depend on its success in providing goods and services for other people. Competition tends to ensure that only those who best satisfy the requirements of their fellows prosper. Incomes partly reflect the success of an organisation in meeting the requirements of consumers who have chosen to pay for the product supplied. Luck may be a factor, but to resent it and to desire coercively to eliminate its effects destroys opportunity. It may be that a company decides to sell a product because of a private obsession of its owner, and that by sheer luck it proves to be a good seller. Nevertheless, the company has been of service to others.

That is, rewards depend on the value of goods and services to the people who choose to buy them, and not only on the personal merits or needs of suppliers. For this reason Hayek regrets that market rewards have sometimes been justified exclusively as the deserved outcome of hard work or skill.[64] Individuals may justly feel proud of their success, he says, but their pride should come from having given good service in the estimation of others, an altogether more humble basis for pride.

Of course, a wise employer will take pains to ensure that relative pay within his company reflects merit, but such decisions are the province of private bargaining, not the legitimate domain of politics.

3. Equality at the Starting Gate

Equality of opportunity can also be a trap. If it means that there should be no artificial obstacles to achievement, the principle is compatible with liberty. Frequently it means no such thing, but equality at the 'starting gate'. It is an inevitable and unavoidable element of the human condition to be born into a particular family and for some families to confer more advantages than others on their offspring. The egalitarian view tends to be that if good parents give a child a better start, the advantage gained is improper because it is not the result of the child's own merit.

Clearly if you are fortunate enough to have well-off parents who buy you extensive private tuition, this confers an initial advantage over other children. But investment by devoted parents is no guarantee of performance and there are many examples of poorly-endowed people rising by their own efforts and of the well-endowed losing their fortunes through incompetence, bad luck or moral failure.

The doctrine of equality at the starting gate leads to demands for the eradication of inherited advantages. Families, instead of being recognised as essential institutions for raising responsible citizens through moral training and developing character, are seen as the source of unfair differences. Parents have a natural desire for their children to succeed but to the egalitarian, this is an 'unfair' advantage which should be removed, cancelled or 'compressed'. If they achieved their aim they would undermine one of the main forces for good in the world, the powerful natural desire of parents to help their children do well. How much harm has the pursuit of equality already done to the family? And if egalitarian measures do undermine the family, have they weakened it as a character-building institution vital to civic harmony? No such question occurs to the egalitarian.

4. The Juxtaposition of Poverty and Wealth

Poverty, it is said, should not exist alongside prosperity, from which it is inferred that the rich have a special obligation to help the less fortunate.

It is true that the wealthy have a special duty to assist the poor. This duty has been central to the Judeo-Christian message and remains as valid today as ever. However, this notion is intermingled with two further sentiments: (i) a sense of envy towards the wealthy and (ii) a desire to use the power of the state to profit at the expense of other people. Together they have provided a rationale for the use of political power to take income and wealth from the 'undeserving rich'.

Envy remains a powerful force. No one, it is said, should be able to buy a privileged education or superior health care. This doctrine is close to the view that people should be equal at the 'starting gate', but is distinct in being based on animosity.

Support for redistributive justice is partly rooted in the desire to relieve hardship, but it also appeals to a rather lower motive, namely the selfishness of voters who are told that they will benefit from taxes imposed on others. This bribery has broken the traditional solidarity of all taxpayers against the profligacy of governments. In Britain our liberties were built on this solidarity as monarchs from the Saxons to the Stuarts and their successors conceded individual rights and constitutional checks in return for taxes. The policy of governments this century has been to divide and rule by telling one section of the population that their benefits are at the expense of 'the rich'. The result has been a higher burden of taxation than ever, and a particularly high burden on the low paid.

Many socialists who base their ethical stance on their alleged animosity to the selfishness ingrained in capitalism, in reality appeal to the very sentiment they claim to detest.

If we are to preserve liberty, political institutions should appeal to the best in people. Encouraging people to believe that they can benefit at the expense of the rich promotes politicised selfishness.

It is sometimes said to be 'obscene' for huge disparities of wealth to exist alongside poverty, and if you said to any cross-section of the population that the wealthy few must give up their luxury cars so that the benefit level could be raised there would be much support, because spending on luxuries is seen as frivolous. The problem is that the total amount of money spent frivolously is small and the end result of redistribution over the last 40 years or so has been the heavy imposition of taxes on people who are far from wealthy and who will never be in a position to buy a Rolls Royce or a Porsche. Far from ending bad or wasteful patterns of life to help the poor, redistribution has meant eroding the income of the low-paid worker.

In any event, much personal spending is not frivolous, and reducing disposable incomes has meant that individuals and families are unable to accumulate savings sufficient, for instance, to invest in capital goods. There is a hidden assumption that the weekly wage represents the cost of physical support plus 'pocket money' for conveniences, from which it follows that there is no harm if the government takes part of it away. But the result has been that many people have too little to invest in capital or to save against contingencies, or to donate to charity, or, many would say, insufficient to spend on the arts. As a result, governments have often assumed responsibility for investment, welfare and cultural spending, adding further to the concentration of power in political hands.

Concern about the juxtaposition of wealth and poverty is sometimes linked to the view that economic activity is a zero-sum game, that is, every gain is judged to be at the expense of someone else. This claim is disproved by economic growth and by the plain fact that voluntary exchanges frequently benefit all parties to the transaction. The zero-sum argument continues to maintain credibility because in any marketplace you can get a buyer's market or a seller's market. For example, if a fruit seller in a street market has a lot of ripe fruit on a Friday afternoon, knowing that the market is closed until Monday and that his produce will go off over the weekend, then he must sell cheap. He finds himself in a buyer's market and in such a case the buyer's gain is at the expense of the seller. And it is possible for a local labour market to be in the same condition, with the result that an individual may be able to command only a low wage for his particular package of skills and character. However, the best safeguard for those in a weak bargaining position is to enjoy freedom of movement and initiative to escape from unwanted low pay or unwanted high (or low) prices. There is, in any event, little chance of governments ever eradicating buyers' or sellers' markets because they are the result of the imbalance of supply and demand, factors under the influence of buyers and sellers, not the authorities.

5. *Positive and Negative Freedom*

Freedom is often confused with power, a tendency encouraged by distinguishing between positive freedom and negative freedom. But according to Hayek, negative freedom is concerned with individual autonomy whilst positive freedom means 'power' and forms part of a wider ideology which wants the power of the state to be used to bring about equality of outcome.

Freedom in the classical-liberal sense describes the absence of an evil, namely coercion by others. As Hayek comments, 'while the uses of liberty are many, liberty is one'. It does not guarantee opportunities:

> In the sense in which we use the term, the penniless vagabond who lives precariously by constant improvisation is indeed freer than the conscripted soldier with all his security and relative comfort. But if liberty may therefore not always seem preferable to other goods, it is a distinctive good that needs a distinctive name.[65]

Hayek is not, therefore, engaging in an argument about the 'real' or 'correct' meaning of the term freedom, he merely wants to avoid equivocation in the use of terms.

Traditionally, advocates of freedom have been concerned with the scope and duties of government. The state plays a key part in preventing private acts of coercion by laying down a framework of rules which it will enforce against private force and fraud. These rules mainly stipulate what you may *not* do to others: kill, steal, break agreements, and so on. But, because it enjoys a monopoly of coercion, the government is also a potential menace to liberty, and this danger explains why classical liberals have been particularly concerned with the rights of the individual against the central power.

In spite of Hayek's careful argument that positive and negative freedom are different things, many socialist writers define freedom as the 'availability of options'. In doing so they fail to see why Hayek values individual autonomy. Hayek's ideal is the thinking, self-improving person and he contends that government restraint through a rule of law is necessary in order to grant people a sphere of action protected against pre-defined acts of coercion at the hands of others.

Socialists call the tradition of freedom which emphasises the rights of the individual against the central power 'negative freedom', to imply that it is inferior compared with positive freedom. We can understand their ploy better by comparing freedom with another concept 'peace'. Peace is also a negative concept because it describes the absence of war.

Imagine that 'negative' peace described a state of affairs in which there was no war and therefore greater opportunities to prosper. It is inevitable that some people would prosper more than others, partly through luck, and partly because some would work harder and invest their money more wisely. Imagine that a political group began to demand 'positive' peace because it objected to the fact that some people reaped higher rewards because of the absence of war.

Peace is a desirable state of affairs in its own right. Positive peace does not mean that there is even less bloodshed than in a state of mere negative peace. The word 'positive' refers to an entirely separate doctrine, equalization.

Moreover, the effect of calling this levelling doctrine 'positive peace' serves to conceal its true character.

The 'positive' freedom sought by socialists who assert their 'social' concern is in reality highly individualistic. Some socialists, those who call themselves 'ethical socialists', have made this criticism powerfully against comrades they call 'egoistic socialists'. The freedom sought by 'egoistic socialists' is that of the isolated individual, who regards everyone else as in his way. Rather like some motorists, everything else, including the legal speed limit and the other drivers, is an obstacle to their will. It hardly needs to be said that no such ethos can serve as a basis for a free society. But is it correct to accuse socialists of adopting a hyper-individualist doctrine of 'freedom as power', when they enthuse about 'society' and campaign against private self-interest?[66] There is in reality no contradiction, because by 'society' they mean politics. Power is the common factor. They see freedom as power, and they see 'the community' or society as concern with the exercise of power. At this point the argument shades into Marxism: politics is about pursuing the interests of one class of individuals at the expense of another. The deliberate confusion of freedom and power by distinguishing between positive and negative freedom is nothing but sophistry calculated to trick the unwary into surrendering their liberty in the name of freedom.

6. Pragmatic Universalism: Coercion of the Middle Class

Some critics object to private education because it means that articulate middle class parents withdraw their children from the local school. If they were forced to stay, socialists argue, then they would use their social skills to raise standards for all pupils. The same argument is applied to private health care. If the middle class are allowed to opt out, they will not try to improve the state system. This argument is closely linked to envy, but with a more pragmatic intent.

First, it is naïve to imagine that if articulate parents are forced to send their children to the local school they will use their energy to raise standards for all. It is more likely that they will concentrate on gaining advantages for their own children, as they have done to date. It is notorious that middle class parents use their incomes to buy homes in suburbs served by high quality schools, a course of action not open to the less well off.

Second, the argument disregards the rebound effect of competition. If parents take their children from one school they send a message, not only to the head of the school they are leaving, but also to other schools. Their action resonates through the whole system. And if several parents leave a particular school, or a waiting list develops for another, the message becomes loud and difficult to avoid. Schools must adjust or disappear.

7. The Wenceslas Myth

The desire for equality is not only the result of envy. It also exploits the human desire to obtain something for nothing, when in reality the benefits are at the general expense. On a recent radio phone-in programme a caller came up with the classic line: 'The government should pay, not the taxpayer'. He plainly assumed that the government had money of its own. Samuel Brittan has called this notion the 'Wenceslas myth' after the 10th century monarch, celebrated in the Christmas carol, who shared some of his own wealth with a poor man gathering winter fuel. It has led to the myth that governments have a choice between being mean or generous, like Good King Wenceslas.[67] It should hardly need to be said that whatever the state does involves taking money from someone else. Yet the myth lingers on.

8. Integrationism or Citizenship Rights

All welfare should be universal as a badge of citizenship. This is sometimes called the 'one nation' view. Those who wish to integrate people through universal benefits believe that their policy will permit every person to become a citizen. Modern citizenship theory owes much to T.H. Marshall, who contended that before the welfare state people acquired political and civil rights to which we should now add 'social' rights, including welfare rights and social services. Social rights give people the right to 'share to the full in the social heritage and to live the life of a civilised being according to the standards prevailing in the society'.[68] More recent advocates of citizenship theory claim that people are excluded from society if they are denied certain consumption opportunities and contend that this gives them a claim on the public purse.[69]

Because the purpose of the welfare state is to integrate people into the community, welfare benefits are not considered to be public charity. They are an entitlement which must be given universally as of right to (a) avoid stigma, (b) compensate victims for misfortune, and (c) enable people to achieve the consumption standard necessary to play their part as full citizens. Means testing, whilst not wholly rejected, is to be avoided because it 'marginalises' the poor.

The weakness of citizenship theory is that its adherents have not understood that universalism intensifies the corruption of vote-buying and middle-class subsidies.[70] Where is the concern for social solidarity in telling people they can enjoy many benefits at the general expense? Far from generating one nation, this breeds division and antagonism and turns the political process into a battleground for consumption at the expense of other people. Professor Richard Titmuss intensely disliked private altruism which he dismissed as involving a 'gratitude imperative'[71] but he did not see the emergence of a political 'gratitude imperative' built on buying votes with promises of spending at the general expense. David Harris, one of the more thoughtful of the citizenship theorists, acknowledges that welfare benefits do not necessarily integrate people. They may have the opposite effect of generating conflict in the sense of a scramble for benefits.[72]

During the post-war years the pursuit of redistributive justice has been closely allied with paternalistic concern for the 'working class' or the 'masses' whose lives need to be organised for them. They need to be compelled to save or insure against various contingencies, such as ill-health and old age. Such paternalism is called horizontal distribution, to make it seem as if its rationale was the same as other forms of redistributive justice, notably vertical redistribution, or taking from the rich to give to the poor. But horizontal redistribution is not taking other people's money, it is taking each individual's own money and forcing him to spend it in a manner determined by the government of the day.

The distinction between corporate association and civil association is once again useful in understanding citizenship theory. Citizenship theorists fail to acknowledge that social solidarity is possible without equality of outcome. People may also feel a bond of loyalty towards institutions which offer a *minimum* without equality. And more important still, people may feel loyalty towards institutions because they provide opportunities for self-development and for making private and unpoliticised contributions to the well-being of others. Citizenship theorists since T.H. Marshall have sought to integrate people into a corporate association. Personal responsibility plays a small part, if any, in their analysis and the powers of government are to be pervasive.

Few socialists have understood precisely how shallow an ideal equality of consumption is. Participation in the community comes to be measured primarily by spending capacity. People are consumers, takers, or satisfaction seekers. Self-improvement and duty to others are nowhere to be found. No less important, the desire to equalise consumption ignores services which are not priced. This diverts attention from aspects of life which are not commercialised such as the mutual support of married couples, the education and care of children within the family, voluntary help given to neighbours and friends, or organised work for voluntary associations. Indeed, much of what makes for a good and fulfilled life is voluntary and unrewarded, and the desire for equalisation has promoted the tendency for the total worth of individuals to be reckoned only in terms of the services for which they receive cash payment.

As Bertrand de Jouvenel remarked, redistributionists think overwhelmingly in terms of consumer satisfaction, and their focus on equating satisfactions distracts them from the reality that there is more to life than consumer satisfaction:

> To the social philosopher interested in human beings it must seem absurd that one should be passionately interested in equalizing among these lives supplies of the 'stuff', on the ground that absorbing the stuff is the stuff of life.[73]

Egalitarians do not understand the entirely different vision of citizenship pursued at the turn of the century. The aim of most reformers during the last half of the 19th century was to improve character. Indeed, the desirability of good character was not at issue between socialists and individualists, as Himmelfarb, Harrison, Collini and other modern historians have noted (below p. 128). T.H. Green had made citizenship central to his philosophy, and his enthusiasm was shared by C.S. Loch of the Charity Organisation Society (COS), who had been one of Green's students. The state, he said:

> cannot afford to have any outcasts or excluded classes, citizens that are not citizens. All are citizens in name; it must see that they are so in reality. It must do its utmost to change the dependent sections of the community into independent.[74]

It was the duty of the state to prevent pauperism, and of 'citizens to give their service to the State for that purpose'. But, the COS had clear views about how the state could best fulfil that duty: by not directing the economic life of citizens, by encouraging individuals to do all they could for themselves, and by leaving space for voluntary institutions to assist the poor without making dependent paupers of them.[75]

The 'university settlement', Toynbee Hall, epitomised the idea of 'citizenship'. Founded in 1884 by Samuel Barnett, it was meant to bridge the gap between the 'two nations' by making better citizens of both—by giving the rich the opportunity to do their duty and the poor the opportunity to realise their potential. It did not dispense relief, or supervise private charity. It provided a place where local people and the residents of Toynbee Hall could come together for meetings, discussions, classes, lectures, concerts and visits. According to Samuel Barnett, the residents were not missionaries bringing the faith to the heathen, nor almoners bringing them money, food, or clothes. They were rather 'settlers' who came to live among the poor—'to learn as much as to teach' and 'to receive as much as to give'.[76]

In 1870 Charles Trevelyan, the civil service reformer and leading member of the COS, explained that one of the purposes of the 'systematic visitation of the poor' encouraged by the COS was to narrow the gulf between the classes: 'to bring back the rich into such close relation with the poor as cannot fail to have a civilising and healing influence, and to knit all classes together in the bonds of mutual help and goodwill.'[77] Today's citizenship theorists, with their focus on spending power, would no doubt find any such approach incomprehensible.

We are now seeing a contest between two competing visions of citizenship: on the one hand the *equalised* citizen and on the other, the *morally-responsible* citizen. Under the former view, the 'good life' is determined by politicians in the political process; whereas under the latter, the role of the state is to facilitate the freedom of individuals to choose the 'good life' for themselves in mutual but voluntary association with other people.

9. Brotherly Love

Equality derives some of its moral force from utopian theories which condemn the pursuit of self-interest and advocate brotherly love. The idea of sharing rather than competing much inspired the early Fabians like Sidney Webb. According to Beatrice Webb, he found in socialism a substitute faith for his lost religious belief.[78] But sharing has worked only where possessions are not simply shared but also disdained altogether as, for instance, in a monastery. Most socialists, however, do not renounce possessions totally. According to Bertrand de Jouvenel, socialism therefore:

> seeks to restore ... unity without the faith which causes it. It seeks to restore sharing as amongst brothers without contempt for worldly goods, without recognition of their worthlessness. It does not accept the view that consumption is a trivial thing, to be kept down to the minimum.[79]

Far from rejecting material things modern socialists want economic growth as much as any capitalist, but they demand greater equality of consumption, a doctrine which requires political action to override individual differences. Their demand for equalised consumption is very different from fraternal sharing.

The reality is that modern theories of redistributive justice take much of their inspiration from the narrowest kind of selfish materialism. Social justice, in the sense of equal consumer satisfaction, hardly deserves to be classified as an ideal at all. As de Jouvenel remarked, 'Nothing quite so trivial has ever been made into a social ideal'.[80]

Socialist writers in recent decades have also been successful in associating markets with selfishness. This propaganda victory is based largely on the confusion of self-interest with selfishness, but not all instances of self-interest are examples of selfishness. Self-regard may be selfish; equally it may not. For example, the extreme form of other-regarding, or altruistic, behaviour rejects all regard to self whatsoever, believing that even to make an effort to feed oneself diverts attention away from service of others or service of God. Mendicant friars lived according to such principles, refraining from work and relying entirely on begging for support. But we cannot all be beggars and it is therefore essential to human survival that most of us take the trouble to support ourselves and our dependents. Not to be self-interested in our own survival involves imposition on others.

In seeking to support ourselves we pursue our self-interest and, since we live in a prosperous society, it is legitimate for us to increase our own comforts as well as merely to provide for necessities. However, we may go about making efforts to support ourselves in a selfish or unselfish manner. And here lies the source of the confusion. Selfishness means consistently putting your own interests *above* those of others or consistently disregarding the interests of others. Self-interest means, at the minimum, providing for yourself instead of relying on others, but to the classical economists it primarily meant seeking to better your own conditions and those of your family. At its minimum it was a permissive doctrine, claiming only that there is no shame in seeking a better life through work, thrift and trade on terms mutually acceptable to others. Whether an individual chooses only to earn sufficient income for self-support and no more, or whether he prefers to exert himself to rise above mere self-sufficiency is a matter of personal preference. But self-interest does not necessarily entail selfishness.

10. Rawls and Rawlsian Variants

John Rawls tries to arrive at a principle of just distribution which might be accepted by everyone if no one knew what position in society he occupied. He suggests that we put ourselves, as it were, outside society in an 'original position' and that in this condition we attempt to establish principles of justice. In this 'original position', which corresponds to the state of nature in social contract theory, no one knows his status, social class, occupation or wealth.[81] No one knows who is advantaged or disadvantaged and, therefore, the argument runs, the principles cannot be devised to favour this or that group of persons.

Rawls' aim is lay down a distributive pattern or end-state favouring the poor which permits a degree of inequality (which he believes to be necessary to encourage productive effort) whilst permitting few sacrifices of 'basic liberties'. There are two principles. First, 'Each person is to have an equal right to the most extensive total system of equal basic liberties compatible with a similar system of liberty for all.' Second, social and economic inequalities are to be arranged so that they are both (a) to the greatest benefit of the least advantaged, consistent with the just savings principle (below); and (b) attached to offices and positions open to all under conditions of fair equality of opportunity. The first principle has priority over the second. According to Rawls, the 'just savings principle' cannot be clearly set out, but it has to do with how much one generation saves in order to benefit subsequent generations. In practice, it appears that the amount to be saved would be settled from time to time by political decision, which means that the principle provides a handy rationale for arbitrary acts of political confiscation. The 'general conception' underlying Rawls' scheme is this: 'All social primary goods—liberty and opportunity, income and wealth, and the bases of self-respect—are to be distributed equally unless an unequal distribution of any or all of these goods is to the advantage of the least favoured'.[82]

Robert Nozick has mounted a fundamental challenge to Rawls' theory. He questions the assumptions taken for granted by Rawls. First, he asks why individuals in Rawls' original position are presumed to choose rules based on groups rather than individuals. Second, he asks why it is assumed that an end-state theory would be preferred, thus ruling out selection of an 'entitlement' or 'historical' theory of justice. And, he asks, why it is obvious that equality of outcome would be preferred. Moreover, Rawls writes as if he believes that total output is primarily a consequence of social co-operation, and because the total product is the result of social co-operation he presumes it is a 'social' (for 'social' read 'political') responsibility to distribute it. According to Nozick, co-operation consists of a sequence of exchanges, and the ensuing total output is wholly accidental. This total product is not, therefore, common property available for political distribution. Why, he asks, 'isn't the appropriate ... set of holdings just the one which *actually occurs* via this process of mutually-agreed-to exchanges whereby people choose to give others what they are entitled to give or hold?'[83] Ultimately, Nozick believes, all patterned theories, of which Rawls' is the most sophisticated, fail to respect the individual.

Hayek also takes issue with Rawls. He criticises the concept of social justice because, by putting each person's material position at the disposal of the government and focusing on the relative position of groups, it provides a basis for the corruption of the democratic process. But he is not wholly opposed to any effort to appraise the overall fairness of a given social order. He urges only that in assessing its fairness or desirability we put aside our awareness of our own material position in it. His alternative method of appraising the 'fairness' of a whole society or culture has much in common with Rawls' technique of deciding on the desirability of a social order from behind a 'veil of ignorance', that is without knowing what our own position in it would be.[84] Essentially Hayek believes that laws should increase the life chances of *unknown* persons:

> All the law can do is to add to the number of favourable possibilities likely to arise for some unknown person and thus to build up an increasing likelihood that favourable opportunities will come anyone's way.[85]

We should, therefore, regard as the most desirable order of society one which we would choose, 'if we know that our initial position in it would be decided purely by chance (such as the fact of our being born into a particular family)'. Put another way, 'the best society would be that in which we would prefer to place our children if we knew that their position in it would be determined by lot'. In these circumstances very few people, he believes, would choose either an egalitarian order, in which the government sought to level each person down to some official standard, or one in which riches were available to the few, as we find in aristocratic societies. Instead, most would choose a liberal-democratic society which offered the great majority the opportunity to thrive by their own efforts and provided an acceptable minimum for the less fortunate.[86] For instance, if you had a chance to live in the eighteenth century and you knew you would be an aristocrat you might find the idea attractive, but if your position in the eighteenth century was to be assigned randomly, the chances are you would be a landless labourer or a servant. A society in which each individual's lifestyle is a matter for personal choice and which offers the prospect, but not the guarantee, of success for all those who are willing to work, is far more appealing.

Rawlsian theories are useful to collectivists because they muddy the water, implying that it is possible to have a little bit of equality without a serious reduction in freedom. Few modern socialists aspire to bring about absolute equality;

rather they believe there is a trade-off between equality and efficiency in maximising output. Typically, they call for equality to be pursued only up to the point at which it is thought consistent with economic efficiency. But the fact remains that it is a rationale for discretionary use of political power. It is significant that egalitarians define the trade-off as one between equality and efficiency. They do so because they see the market as chiefly a technique for wealth production. For them, it is primarily an incentive system which can be used in a socialist society to generate wealth. I have already argued that the system of voluntary exchange cannot be understood except as part of a wider moral, legal and spiritual setting. It is another example of socialists slipping into the habit of which they accuse free marketeers. They see men as rational calculators, responding to incentives, not as free persons guided by morals, affected by duties and influenced, but not controlled, by incentives.

The focus of socialists on material equality enables them to see that material incentives are functional because they encourage people to exert themselves and thus to create economic growth. But it diverts their attention from a bigger reality, namely that it is the ethos of personal responsibility which is the real engine driving economic growth. Professor Raymond Plant (now Lord Plant) is a typical exponent of this revised 'market socialism'. When speaking of the process whereby wealth is first created and then finds its way into the pockets of individuals and families, Plant uses the term 'trickle down', a notion which suggests a movement of money from the wealthy to the poor, and which conjures up an image of the poor receiving crumbs from the rich man's table. Is this an accurate way of thinking about the ideas articulated by the classical economists?

It is important to understand the nature of the societies the classical economists were hoping to escape from. The old medieval order was hierarchical and static. Most people lived at subsistence level, year in year out, and from generation to generation. And most were born to a particular station in life. In rural areas there were few choices to be made: the village meeting in some localities or the lord of the manor in others, dictated which crops must be grown, when ploughing must begin, when to sow, which animals might be tended, and so on. In the towns the guilds exercised detailed control over all aspects of work, including the products that could be made, the prices charged, the quantities produced and the methods, tools and materials that might be used.

By the seventeenth and eighteenth centuries it was possible to detect a fundamental change that had been slowly gathering pace for three to four hundred years, but which was not fully understood until the later part of the eighteenth century. Families, initially dotted here and there, later in larger numbers, began to defy the old ways. They used their practical wisdom to improve the methods used to grow crops, rear animals and make useful goods for others to use. Dependent only on their courage and what today we might call their human capital, they defied the village authorities and tried new ways of farming, or they left for new localities where traditional authority was weak. Similarly, some families left the stifling atmosphere of the ancient boroughs for rural areas where the writ of the guilds did not run. Here they tried their hands at different methods of manufacture and trade. As it turned out, these pioneers prospered. Following tradition in agriculture, animal husbandry and manufacturing created a static, hierarchical life at subsistence level for all but a few aristocrats. But when individuals were set free to develop their own methods of farming and manufacture by trial-and-error, economic growth was the outcome. Prosperity began to spread as each began to share in the new prosperity created by the application of human initiative and knowledge.

The essence of this revolutionary departure from the old order was free scope for human ingenuity, which in turn assumes that individuals are taking personal responsibility for their own affairs, in religious and moral matters no less than in their work. The same families that took risks in growing crops in new ways or making products by different methods also tended to prefer to elect their own preachers in a general meeting rather than to countenance the authority of bishops. And in hard times, they preferred the mutual aid of the church congregation or the friendly society to dependency on the poor law.

Thus, the new prosperity which enabled the vast majority to escape from the old, unchanging, hierarchical social order was the result of individuals who were willing to take risks by applying their own practical knowledge in their work. But consider the attitude of modern egalitarians. They show no awareness of the centrality of personal responsibility, human ingenuity and human capital in generating prosperity. The egalitarian's eyes are focused on relative rewards and whether they are deserved. If talent gives rise to a higher income, they are concerned to impose a penalty, particularly if the talent is natural or has been encouraged by attentive parents. They do not understand that personal responsibility is the determining factor.

To sum up: the idea of social justice strikes many as, at worst, harmless and at best thoroughly desirable. However, experience of pursuing equality of outcome this century, not only in communist countries, shows that it is incompatible with a society of free individuals. Market competition should not be looked upon merely as a device for creating wealth which can then be parcelled out in the political process. It is inseparable from a wider vision of a society of thinking, choosing, and morally responsible citizens.

Hayek was inspired by the ideal of a free society in which individuals, in mutual concert with their fellows, could conceive and pursue their own version of the good life, thus enabling unknown persons to contribute to the good of others by innovation or achievement in industry, services, the arts and voluntary work. His ideal was to maximise the chances for everyone to live a full life in all its dimensions. In contrast, the egalitarian's focus is narrow and material. Perhaps without being fully aware of it, they see people merely as consumers, and desire only to equalise their power to consume material goods. Civil society is far more than a system of economic rewards.

From reactions to *Equalising People*[87] I know that this line of reasoning will anger those who see the pursuit of 'social justice' as a kind of middle way between the old statist socialism and unfettered capitalism. And to a degree the pursuit of partial equality is preferable to absolute equalization, but the question remains: why use the power of the state to equalise incomes at all? There is a strong case for using the powers of government to prevent hardship, but once poverty has been eliminated why should the government concern itself in any way with the incomes people have?

Corporate Association: Conclusions

The rationales for corporate association typically present themselves as 'democratic' or respectful of the individual, but in reality they enjoin us to surrender up the power of self-government to leaders. The intellectual elite, which presumes that it will lead, promises to serve 'the people', but it defines 'the people' as creatures who need to have things done for them. The ideal of social justice, for example, promises to remove our main cares and to ensure that our chief material wants are supplied. The conception of people as victims, now so prevalent among social policy analysts, appears to be based on sympathy, but defines people as incapable of coping without political or expert assistance.

Thus, corporate association appeals to two personality types: first, those who imagine they will be the leaders; and second, those who welcome the release from life's cares promised by the leaders.

The tendency of all such doctrines is to weaken human character by diminishing opportunities for us to develop our skills and our virtues, qualities which can only be acquired through direct participation in overcoming the hazards of life. Civil association, by contrast, is intended to equip us for self-rule not political rule, that is, for non-political co-operation in joint endeavours. In doing so, it increases opportunities for us to be of service to others, whereas corporate association diminishes such opportunities and thus reduces our potential to grow as people, rendering us still more in need of paternalistic guidance. Modern advocates of corporate association aim to rule. They are the modern equivalent of the demagogues of old who needed followers, but who preferred to manipulate their supporters rather than to respect them.

Thus, five rationales for collectivism have been identified. All have one theme in common: they provide grounds for the authorities to supervise individual lives. All assume that the state is a corporate association, rather than a civil association.

4

The Welfare System: What is Going Wrong?

THIS chapter is organised as follows. First, I will describe the arguments of leading American contributors to the welfare debate, for it was American scholars who first began successfully to put forward radical criticisms of the harmful effects of welfare in the late 1970s. Their analyses struck a chord with many in Britain.

Second, I will focus on Charles Murray's claim that Britain is repeating American mistakes, leading to the development of an underclass, and above all to the breakdown of the family.

Third, I will describe the criticisms now being made by socialists, including Frank Field, Norman Dennis and David Selbourne. And finally, I will offer an interpretation of the welfare problem in the light of Oakeshott's three inseparables.

The Evolving Welfare Debate: Lessons From America

Since the late 1970s two main types of criticism of welfare have evolved. The first tendency has been to understand the problem as one of incentives. The argument has been that the welfare system made payments if people fulfilled certain conditions, with the outcome that some altered their behaviour to qualify. Instead of working to escape poverty, they refrained from work because they received as much income (or more) out of work. Analysts who regard perverse incentives to be the problem have urged the devising of new systems which produce different incentives. This was the approach, for instance, of Milton and Rose Friedman in *Free to Choose* when they advocated a negative income tax scheme.

In the view of Milton and Rose Friedman, most welfare programmes should never have been enacted. Without them, many beneficiaries would have been self-reliant individuals instead of wards of the state and they propose a scheme to bring about an orderly transfer of people from 'welfare rolls to payrolls'.[1] They recommend the replacement of the existing 'ragbag of specific programmes' by a single comprehensive programme of income support in cash which would be integrated with income tax.[2] The disadvantage of a personal tax allowance is that if an individual earns less than the allowance, it is useless. Under the Friedmans' negative income tax scheme, if a person's income falls below the level of his personal tax allowance he receives a payment from the tax authorities equivalent to the difference between his allowance and his actual income (or some percentage of the difference). In this manner the incentive to work will be retained.

Martin Anderson can also be included in the 'incentives' camp, but he recognised that financial incentives would not be enough to encourage some people to work, and argued that they should be *required* to work as a condition of benefits.[3]

The second tendency believed that the behavioural changes that emerged during the 1960s—rising crime, disinclination to work and family breakdown—could not be understood *only* as a result of the benefit system. It was necessary to question some of the other cultural signals associated with the 1960s. In *Beyond Entitlement* Lawrence Mead criticised the deterministic approach that guided policy makers and stressed the importance of personal responsibility. However, he believed that a federal welfare scheme could be devised to avoid the unwanted effects of earlier measures. Mead's argument is significant because it emphasises the importance of character as well as external incentives. Also significant in the emerging debate was George Gilder's *Wealth and Poverty* (1981), *Out of the Poverty Trap* by Stuart Butler and Anna Kondratis of the Heritage Foundation (1987), and *The New Consensus on Family and Welfare*, edited by Michael Novak, also published in 1987.

Charles Murray tends to be associated with the 'incentives' approach and some of his reasoning is of that type, but his argument is more complex. In *Losing Ground* he argued that poverty had worsened, and family breakdown and crime had risen, because of the withdrawal of respect for work, family duty and law-abidingness. The benefit system is one, but only one, of the means by which disrespect for such values has been signalled. The welfare system also has what James Q. Wilson and Richard Herrnstein called 'tutelary' effects. That is, the very act of paying or not paying a benefit sends a signal of approval or disapproval. When the state began to send cash to unmarried mothers to raise their own children instead of sending a social worker to encourage them to have their babies adopted by other couples able to give them a better chance, the moral message changed. Public policies convey moral messages in addition to producing incentive effects. Good conduct, according to Wilson and Herrnstein, is based on 'internalised inhibitions, reinforced by social sanctions' and public policies are among the signals of approval or disapproval being transmitted.[4]

This means that how much we spend on welfare may be less important than the type of behaviour reinforced by the spending. Do we, for instance, reward acceptance of responsibility or do we reward its opposite?[5] In a separate work, Wilson cites the changing take-up rate of Aid to Families with Dependent Children (AFDC) as evidence of a cultural shift. In 1967, 63 per cent of persons eligible for AFDC claimed it; by 1970 91 per cent claimed. In short, he says, 'the character of persons changed'. Previously they had regarded welfare as 'a temporary and rather embarrassing expedient', but they came to see it as a right.[6] This change coincided with daily bombardment of the poor by that very message.

Charles Murray's Criticisms of US Welfare

Before the New Deal reforms of the 1930s, assistance of the poor in America was local and voluntary. In 1935 AFDC and Unemployment Insurance were introduced under the impact of the Depression. These early programmes were widely believed to be consistent with liberty, and until the Great Society programmes of 1964-1967, the aim of social policy had been the removal of barriers, in the belief that the poor would rise by their own efforts once given the chance. No one doubted that, once opportunities were created, individuals would seize them. But during the Great Society era such thinking was tacitly abandoned as the emphasis shifted to making direct transfers of cash to the poor. The mere removal of obstacles was no longer thought sufficient.

Aid to Families with Dependent Children (AFDC), introduced in 1935, was limited to the aged, blind people and lone parents, mostly widows. Unemployment Insurance was introduced at the same time, but it was not seen as welfare. It was financed from local payroll taxes, and benefits were an entitlement. Depending on the particulars of each state scheme, payments were generally for a limited duration of 26 weeks, subject to previous earnings and length of employment. It was to tide people over while they found new work. According to Charles Murray, the traditional consensus was beginning to crumble in the late 1950s, and between 1964 and 1967 social policy changed from:

> the dream of ending the dole to the institution of permanent income transfers that embraced not only the recipients of the dole but large new segments of the American population. It went from the ideal of a color blind-society to the reinstallation of legalized discrimination. They were polar changes that were barely recognised as such while they were happening.[7]

At first, the front runners were programmes to add directly to the skills at the disposal of the poor and thus strengthen their hand in the labour market. Head Start, for instance, was a pre-school programme for disadvantaged children.

But the record of these programmes was disappointing. Individuals completed training schemes but continued to be out of work. Often they remained ill-suited to all but the lowest-paid positions, jobs which they had been encouraged to see as beneath them. Reformers reacted to the failure of these programmes in a piecemeal way, and sought to devise new incremental measures by which governments could raise the living standards of the poor. By the late 1960s the view was increasingly taken that if training did not work, the poor must be assisted by direct income transfers. Later measures to introduce a guaranteed income, such as the Nixon Family Assistance Plan, were defeated, but other measures had a similar effect, such as Food Stamps (1964), Medicaid (1965), and Supplemental Security Income (SSI) (1972). Until 1962 AFDC was confined to single parents, but in that year states were permitted to provide for two-parent families under the AFDC-UP (for Unemployed Parent) option. By 1987, 26 states and the District of Columbia had taken up the option.[8] The result of these and similar measures was that federal spending on the needy grew in real terms by more than 10 per cent a year between 1965 and 1974.

Despite these huge outlays, it gradually became clear that the number of people in poverty was not falling. It was not that the poor suffered the same degree of privation as in years gone by; it was rather that dependence on the state had become a fixed way of life for millions of Americans. The aim of reformers had been to release the poor, so that they might become self-directing citizens; but the reality was that they had created a dependent population.

What was also significant about the evolving policy changes of the 1960s was that, imperceptibly, the poor had come to be seen in a wholly different light. They were no longer free citizens just waiting to be given their chance, but passive victims whose lives could be adjusted through the administration of government schemes. To return to Oakeshott's language, the earlier assumptions had been consistent with civil association, whereas the 1960s ethos assumed corporate association, that is the central direction of followers by leaders.

Murray contrasts the situation in 1950 with 1980. Government health and medical expenditures in 1980 were six times the 1950 figure; public assistance cost thirteen times more; education expenditure was 24 times higher; social insurance, 27 times more; and housing, 129 times more.[9] But in spite of these dramatic increases in expenditure, poverty appeared undiminished. When the Food Stamp programme got under way in 1965 it served 424,000 persons. By 1968 there were 2.2 million beneficiaries; and by 1980, the number had grown to over 21 million, fifty times the original figure and ten times the number at the end of the Johnson administration.[10] In 1968, when Johnson left office, 13 per cent of the US population was classified as poor; yet by 1980, after expenditure on social welfare had quadrupled, 13 per cent of the population remained poor.[11]

Unemployment rates appeared to have worsened for some groups. In 1954, 85 per cent of black males aged 16 and over were participating in the labour force, only slightly lower than the proportion for whites. From 1966 black male labour force participation started to fall faster than white participation. By 1972 there was a gap of 5.9 per cent, and by 1976, 7.7 per cent.[12]

Family breakdown, too, had accelerated. From 1950 to 1963 black illegitimate births rose slowly from about 17 per cent of all black births to 23 per cent. In 1980, 48 per cent of live births among blacks were to single women.[13]

The link between, on the one hand, welfare and, on the other, work effort and family dissolution, is demonstrated by the income maintenance experiments conducted in Seattle and Denver between 1971 and 1978. Negative income tax was a favourite scheme of reformers, especially economists in the tradition of Milton Friedman, until the income maintenance experiments. Families in the programme were guaranteed incomes ranging from 50 to 135 per cent of the poverty line. If they worked, the grant was reduced by between 30 and 70 per cent of earnings, in the belief that this gave them an 'incentive' to keep or take a job. The results were compared with those for families who had access only to normal welfare benefits.

The Seattle and Denver studies revealed that husbands reduced their hours worked by about 5 per cent, wives (in two-parent families) by 15 per cent, and female heads of family by 12 per cent.[14] The most striking effect was on young males who were not heads of families. They reduced their hours of work by 43 per cent if they remained 'non-heads' throughout the study and 33 per cent on average if they married during the study. Most of the reduced work effort was due to some people, particularly wives and young males who were not yet heads of families, dropping out of work altogether. NIT also appeared to encourage family dissolution. In the Seattle and Denver experiments, dissolution of marriages was 36 per cent higher for whites receiving NIT, and 42 per cent higher for blacks.[15]

Why did poverty not diminish as a result of the Great Society programmes? According to Charles Murray, there were two processes at work which led to the undermining of self-reliance. First, 'Status was withdrawn from the low-income, independent working family, with disastrous consequences to the quality of life of such families'. Second, status was also withdrawn from 'the behaviours that engender escape from poverty'.[16]

Lawrence Mead

Murray was associated with the free-market end of the political spectrum, but his concern was not confined to Republicans. Lawrence Mead was identified with the Democrats and shared much of Murray's analysis. The assumption of reformers, he argues, was that all social problems were due to 'denials of freedom', or the presence of barriers, particularly racial. By the mid-1980s, however, the problem was that, after the civil rights reforms of the 1960s, there were no further formidable social barriers which explain the persistence of poverty. Modern social problems, writes Mead, are '*not*, on the whole, due to oppression'.[17] A lot of unemployment has more to do with the 'functioning problems of the jobless themselves than with economic conditions'. The administrators of federal training programmes, he says, find that their clients have 'more difficulty keeping jobs than finding them'.[18]

Mead singles out for special criticism the 'sociological approach'. Its adherents believe that the social sciences can be as quantified and predictive as the natural sciences, and underlying their view is 'environmental determinism', the notion that the events being studied are 'caused' by outside forces. Thus, school failure and crime were said to be 'caused' by material deprivation. The purpose of sociological reasoning, according to Mead, 'was exactly to exempt those at the bottom of society from responsibility for their condition'.[19] Combined with the experimental ethic this meant that:

> Planners had to keep coming up with new programs until they found something that 'worked', that is, some benefit to which poverty responded without obligating the poor themselves.[20]

He is describing the mentality of victimism discussed in Chapter 3. Some economists have also been prone to environmental determinism. Because they are inclined to interpret human behaviour as the result of people pursuing their own interests, they tend to believe that conduct can be changed by adjusting material incentives. A particular result of this type of reasoning is that the less tangible aspects of social problems tend to be played down in favour of the material dimensions which can be quantified. Much analysis consists of relating measurable problems like low income to apparent 'causes' that are also measurable. Generally, causal variables are confined to characteristics of people already collected by the government—age, sex, race, income, benefit claims, etc. The result is that economic analysis has often reinforced the 'sociological' approach: 'The measurable forces that surround the poor, such as inadequate income, education, or employment, are presumed to shape their behaviour in some irresistible way'.[21] But, according to Mead, some types of behaviour, such as paying taxes or low-wage work, can never be made to serve the self-interest of individuals in the narrow economic sense, so that no amount of adjusting incentives will be sufficient. He concludes that certain duties must, therefore, 'be enforced bureaucratically'.[22]

The assumption made by Great Society policy analysts was that 'society' was at fault, but according to Mead:

> Behaviour stems in the first instance from the individual, and there is no way to change it unless at least some responsibility

is imputed to the individual. The assumption of social responsibility blocked policy makers from recognizing those problems, let alone solving them.[23]

Great Society programmes failed to overcome poverty because 'they largely ignored behavioural problems among the poor'. In particular, they omitted to tell clients that they ought to behave differently.[24] The Great Society focused on raising groups, like blacks, relative to others, but according to Mead: 'The underclass cannot be made middle-class in a single generation, except at the cost of government guarantees that deprive the achievement of meaning'.[25]

Although Mead favours a more interventionist government than full-blooded conservatives prefer, he is conscious of the danger of unlimited government power. He therefore tries clearly to define the extent to which the government may obligate its citizens. He lists five main duties:

1. Heads of families, unless aged or disabled, and other adult members of families should work in available jobs.
2. Every person should contribute all that they can to the support of their family.
3. Every citizen should be fluent and literate in English, whatever their native tongue.
4. Children should learn enough in school to be employable.
5. Each citizen should be law-abiding, that is they should be both obedient to law and show general respect for the rights of others.[26]

The most significant reform proposed by Mead is that recipients of welfare should be under an obligation to work. He is unsympathetic to the argument that to compel people to take dull jobs is 'degrading', not very different from condemning them to slavery. According to Mead, work should be undertaken out of a sense of obligation, not for enjoyment, and the unemployed should, therefore, be required to take any legal job that they are 'physically able to do'.[27] Moreover, he points out that present arrangements are unfair to people who already work, possibly doing chores like scrubbing floors. They are paying taxes to support the idle.[28]

But how can this duty be enforced? It is plainly preferable if people work out of a sense of personal responsibility; and indeed no free society could function unless a sense of duty was widely and freely accepted. Most people have such a duty inculcated by private organisations such as family, friends, and the church, but the problem of the poor is that they are dependent on government and, according to Mead, there is, therefore, no alternative to a government role in socialising them. For those who still recoil from his argument, Mead points out that the view he advocates is, and has been, widely supported. If it was abandoned during the 1960s and 1970s, it was only then discarded by intellectuals, not by the population at large. The political problem in social policy is, therefore, not to create *new* standards but, 'to *elevate* into social policy those that already prevail outside the public sector'.[29]

Mead returned to his theme in 1992 with *The New Politics of Poverty*, partly to defend his view against collectivists who said that there were too few job opportunities. He showed that 'unskilled jobs' suitable for the poor were 'widely available'. The main distinction between collectivists and classical liberals was no longer so much over the size of government but 'on whether the needy can be responsible for themselves and, above all, on whether they have the competence to manage their lives'. He found that collectivists, who claim to champion the needy, have a more pessimistic attitude than classical liberals.[30]

The Impact of the Counter Culture

The analyses of the mid-1980s typified by Mead and Murray have been supplemented by powerful more recent studies of cultural change and its impact on welfare. In *The Dream and the Nightmare* Myron Magnet points out that during the 1980s 18.4 million jobs, skilled and unskilled, were created in America, offering escape routes to anyone with the discipline to work. Why, asks Magnet, if the jobs exist, does poverty persist? Poverty, he concludes, is less economic and more cultural. The Have-Nots lack the inner resources to seize their chance and, worse still, as parents they pass on self-defeating values to their children.[31]

The principal reason is that the libertarian collectivist élite who shape mainstream culture have abandoned respect for the values which alone allow the poor to escape their predicament. The culture of the underclass, he says, is like a dialect shaped by mainstream culture. His central argument is that:

> the Haves are implicated because over the last thirty years they radically remade American culture, turning it inside out and upside down to accomplish a cultural revolution whose most mangled victims turned out to be the Have-Nots.[32]

The Haves wanted liberation for themselves as well as the Have-Nots, but succeeded only on their own behalf. The War on Poverty and later measures were intended to 'liberate' the black and poor from poverty. At the same time, the Haves sought to 'liberate' themselves from convention. But, as Chapter 2 showed, they were guided by the concept of freedom as power, that is, they saw freedom as the removal of all obstacles to human desires. Perhaps it was the result of intellectual error rather than calculated self-interest but, either way, freedom as power proved very serviceable to the Haves, for it allowed them to claim that their self-interest coincided with the interests of the poor, thus supplying them with moral credentials for self-indulgence.[33]

Their twin liberations had two effects, according to Magnet. First, he shares Charles Murray's view that respect was withdrawn from behaviour that provided the only escape route from poverty.[34] The ethos of honest achievement through hard work came to be mocked. But, says Magnet, that is all the poor have. A man who starts with little cash and who has little ability must make the most of his character. He cannot command a good job because of his intelligence or skills, but he can make himself indispensable to an employer or to customers by making the most of his main assets: virtues like hard work, loyalty and honesty. The intellectuals who mock menial, dead-end jobs mock the inevitable lot of many of their fellows and they belittle the chief means of advancement open to them. Magnet writes movingly of the injustice done to honest, hard-working people by the supercilious upper crust, who claim to be on their side, but in reality hold them in contempt. He gives the example of a married couple, one of whom works as a janitor while the other makes beds at the local motel. If both earned only the minimum wage, they could support their family of five just above the poverty line. But you do not judge people's lives, he says, only by their income:

> Suppose that these two have brought up their children to respect the parents' hard work, to be curious about the world, to study in school, to take pleasure in family and community life, to consider themselves worthwhile people, to work hard and think about the future, to become skilled tradesmen or even professionals as adults, and to bring grandchildren to visit.

If this is a dead end rather than a human accomplishment worthy of honour, says Magnet, then 'it is hard to know what human life is about'. What message are people to get if they are described as 'chumps and jerks—that their achievement isn't to be valued and indeed is sneered at?'[35]

Second, says Magnet, not only was respect for humble but honest work withdrawn, the poor were also told that they were victims and thus robbed of responsibility for their own actions. Instead of being told that they should seize the available opportunities, they were taught that society was unjust and that they were entitled to be better off, not on their own merits, but as compensation for the wrongs they had suffered.

And there were ample opportunities for people to work their way out of poverty. It is true that pay for low-skill jobs fell. Between 1979 and 1988 the real earnings of white males aged 25-34 lacking a high school diploma fell 18.8 per cent. But there were ample jobs. The availability of jobs requiring more than basic skills increased during the 1980s, but about two in every five jobs created between 1983 and 1990 were unskilled or low skilled. Clerks, cashiers, cooks and light-truck drivers ranked 3rd, 4th, 5th and 6th in the list of jobs created. Labourers and machine operators, 10th and 11th and child-care 14th. These figures exclude off-the-books domestic work which is known to be substantial.[36]

To make matters worse, the libertarian collectivists—or what Norman Dennis calls the egoistic socialists—believed they were pursuing a crusade. They felt their lives had moral content and they did not see themselves as self-indulgent, but as the champions of the poor. Social policy, says Magnet, took on an aspect of faith:

> It invested policies designed to achieve these aims with the zeal that charged the aims themselves. Yet however creditable, that zeal made it hard to argue against the wisdom or efficacy of the specific policies. How could one argue against benevolence and goodwill?[37]

This attitude, which pervaded British social policy intellectuals as much as American, made it especially hard for adherents to confront the failure of their policies, for they gave the Haves their sense of self-worth. The result has been defence of racial quotas, excusing criminals as victims rather than wrongdoers, and uncritical support of never-married mothers regardless of how well they are bringing up their children. In other words, morally indefensible policies came to be defended with moral zeal.

To sum up: the welfare system has had perverse effects on the behaviour of some people, including the encouragement of abstention from work and family breakdown, but it is not the only causal factor. The moral messages conveyed by opinion formers have reinforced the irresponsibility embodied in the welfare system. Over the years, the two factors have acted upon each other, but they are independent variables. Perhaps the relative weakness of the counter-culture in some European countries, like Germany, explains why family breakdown there is less prevalent despite the pervasive welfare systems typical of continental Europe.

Is Britain Repeating American Mistakes?

Charles Murray's first study of Britain, *The Emerging British Underclass,*[38] argued that there are three measures of an underclass in the making: illegitimacy, violent crime, and economic inactivity among men of working age. In his second study, *Underclass: The Crisis Deepens,*[39] he concentrates on family breakdown as the most serious problem, not least because children socialised in broken families are more prone to criminal activity and diminished work effort.

Family Breakdown

Charles Murray focuses especially on illegitimacy as a measure of an underclass in the making. He considers it a more serious sign of breakdown than divorce because there has been no committed father from the outset. The evidence, however, is that when couples divorce whilst they still have dependent children the impact on the children is serious and long-lasting.

Illegitimacy: All societies have tried to ensure that children are raised by both parents and, in particular, to prevent fathers from escaping responsibility. During the first half of this century the percentage of births out of wedlock in Britain remained at around 4 to 5 per cent, with the exception of the period around both World Wars. During World War One it peaked at 6 per cent, and fell back during the inter-war years. During World War Two, illegitimacy reached 9 per cent and then fell again in the early 1950s to the historically typical 5 per cent.

As late as 1961 only 6 per cent of all births occurred outside marriage. In 1971 the figure was still only 8 per cent. By 1981 it had climbed to 13 per cent, but during the 1980s children were born with increasing frequency outside marriage, accounting by 1991 for over 30 per cent of all births. In 1992 the figure was 31 per cent.[40]

The illegitimate births reflect an even higher number of conceptions. In 1991 there were 854,000 conceptions, 44 per cent of which were outside marriage. Nineteen per cent of the conceptions ended in abortion, but the abortion rate is much higher for the unmarried. More than one in three such conceptions ended in abortion.[41]

How does illegitimacy in Britain compare with other countries? Denmark has a huge rate of 46 per cent, France is similar to Britain on 33 per cent. But the German figure is only 15 per cent, Italy 7 per cent, and Greece 3 per cent.[42]

Britain is above the 1991 US figure of 30 per cent. However, the rate for American blacks is far worse than the US average. In 1950 illegitimacy among US blacks was 17 per cent. In 1965, when Daniel Patrick Moynihan wrote *The Negro Family* to warn that family breakdown was diminishing the prospects for black advancement, it was 25 per cent. By 1982 it was 57 per cent and by 1991, 68 per cent. In some inner city areas at least 80 per cent of black children are born out of wedlock. The white figure has also been rising. In 1960 it was 2.3 per cent, but it had risen to 22 per cent by 1991.[43] The figure for all Americans was 30 per cent in 1991, having been only 5.3 per cent in 1960.

Some commentators argue that this trend is not significant because a higher proportion of illegitimate births in Britain is being registered by both parents. It is claimed that this joint registration shows that the relationships are stable even though they lack the 'piece of paper' known as marriage. In 1982 illegitimacy was 14 per cent, and 60 per cent of births were registered by both parents. In 1992, when illegitimacy was over 30 per cent, 76 per cent were registered by both parents, so on the face of it there has been an increase in joint registrations. However, of the joint registrations in 1992, 27 per cent gave *different* addresses, suggesting a relationship less stable than marriage.[44] If the 27 per cent are taken out, 55 per cent were jointly registered at the same address.

But this still leaves a majority who gave the same address, most of whom were co-habiting. Is co-habitation equal to marriage? Kathleen Kiernan found, using data from the National Child Development Study, that women who had their first child within a cohabiting union were less likely to be living with their partner at age 33 than those who had a child within marriage: 37 per cent compared with 58 per cent. Many had formed second or subsequent partnerships.[45]

Moreover, even when cohabitation was followed by marriage, the unions proved less stable than those not preceded by cohabitation. According to *Social Trends* (1994), despite the claim that trial marriages provide a more sound foundation, couples who cohabited before marriage have proved *more* likely to divorce than couples who did not. Of couples first married in the early 1980s, those who lived together before marriage were 50 per cent more likely to have divorced after 5 years and 60 per cent more likely after 8 years.[46]

Divorce: The number of divorces did not exceed 1,000 per year until 1914, and did not exceed 10,000 until 1942. In 1961 27,000 divorces were granted. By 1971, the first year of the operation of the 1969 Divorce Reform Act, the figure had reached 80,000. By 1993 the number of divorces had risen to 173,000, more than double the 1971 figure.[47]

In 1993, 175,961 160,000 children under 16 in England and Wales were affected by divorce. A further 20,500 children aged 16 or over were affected.[48] The British divorce rate of 13 per 1,000 existing marriages is lower than in America, where it is 21, but higher than France where it is 8 and Germany where it is 9.

The following table shows divorce rates in European countries expressed as a number per 1,000 existing population rather than per 1,000 existing marriages.

Table 1
Divorce Per 1000 Population

Denmark	2.5
Netherlands	2.0
France	1.9
West Germany	1.7
Belgium	2.2
Greece	0.6
Italy	0.5
Irish Republic	0.0
United Kingdom	3.0

Source: *Social Trends*, 1995, p. 35.

Lone Parenthood and Dependency: In 1960 9 per cent of children in the United States lived in one-parent homes; by 1991 it was 29 per cent. In Britain in 1971 about 8 per cent of families with dependent children were headed by a lone parent, but by 1992 about 21 per cent of British families with dependent children were one-parent.[49] In 1992 there were about 1.4 million one-parent families in Britain containing about 2.3 million dependent children, some 17 per cent of all dependent children.[50]

About 8 per cent of lone parents in 1992 were men. Widows have declined in number since 1971 to 4 per cent in 1992. The proportion of female lone parents due to separation and divorce was 59 per cent in 1992 and the number of unmarried lone mothers grew slowly until the late 1980s, when it grew rapidly to 29 per cent.[51]

But the one-parent family is partly a propaganda category rather than one which clarifies the nature of recent change. It includes parents who are victims as well as parents who are responsible in whole or in part for falling short of the ideal of the two-parent family. It includes widows, for instance, who have traditionally and rightly enjoyed universal sympathy as the victims of a tragic loss of a husband and father. But many lone parents have wilfully or casually created new human life without proper consideration of the child's best interests.

In the UK about 40 per cent of lone parents work and 60 per cent rely on state welfare benefits. For the never-married group, 93 per cent rely on benefits. In May 1993, the total number of children aged 17 or under receiving income support in one-parent families was 1,850,000.[52]

Number of Lone Parents Receiving Income Support 1988-1993 (thousands)

	1988	1989	1990	1991	1993
All	727	771	812	895	1048
Male Headed	32	34	38	43	59
Female Headed	694	737	774	852	989
Never-Married Female	288	322	347	397	464

Source: Social Security Statistics 1992, p. 26; *Social Security Statistics 1994*, p. 24.

The total cost of income support for lone parents in financial year 1992-93 was 6.6 billion, about 9 per cent of the total social security budget. Annual estimates are made of the duration of lone parents' reliance on state benefits. In May 1993, some 55 per cent had relied on state benefits for two years or more.

Frank Field's analysis of the change in the composition of those receiving national assistance or income support provides another measure of the relative impact of family breakdown.

Table 2
Dependants Reliant on National Assistance/Income Support

	1962	1993
NI Pensioners/Elderly	53	21.0
Unemployed	18	34.0
Sick/Disabled	11	9.0
Lone Parents	-	29.0
Widows	4	0.3
Others Under Pension Age	14	7.0

Source: Field, p. 81.

Field goes on to compare unemployment and lone parenthood as causes of child poverty. In 1984 more children relied on income support because of unemployment than family breakdown. By 1988, family breakdown had become the biggest cause of children relying on income support, and by 1993 lone parenthood was twice as significant as unemployment.

Table 3
Children Reliant on Income Support

	1984	1988	1993
Lone Parents	811,000	1.2m	1.7m
Unemployment	1.1m	783,000	832,000

Source: Field, pp. 83-84.

The Causes of Family Breakdown

Two main explanations of family breakdown have been offered, one stressing the incentive effect, the other cultural change. Patricia Morgan has shown how marriage just does not pay for some groups.[53] Using Morgan's figures, Charles Murray explains the impact of the welfare system on marriage by describing the predicament of a fictitious, honest young couple called Ross and Stacey, who are in their late teens. Stacey has discovered she is pregnant. She and Ross, says Murray, sit down and have a talk:

> Ross has a job paying £228 a week (close to the median for manual workers in 1991, and better than most unskilled young men just getting started). After taking into account deductions for income tax, national insurance, rent and community charges, then adding in their family credit and all other pertinent means-tested or universal benefits, Ross and Stacey and the baby will have an after-tax net of about £152.

But if they do not get married, they will have £216. There will be £74 in benefit for Stacey and the baby, tax free, plus Ross's after-tax income as a single unmarried person, which amounts to about £142. Their weekly premium for not marrying is £64 a week, £3,328 a year, a 'raise', as Murray puts it, of 42 per cent over their married income.[54]

Murray points out that if Ross was unemployed, Stacey would have even less incentive to marry. He is worth less as a husband than as a live-in lover:

> Adding up the income support for a couple with one infant and the family premium, they would have £94 a week, plus a council flat. But if they *don't* get married, the same benefit package will amount to £108—a difference of £14 a week. Little as it may seem to those for whom such sums are pocket money, it amounts to a raise of 15 per cent over the income they would have if they married.

There are other advantages to claiming income support separately. For instance, if Stacey wants to supplement her income after the baby is born, the first £15 of her earnings will be disregarded when calculating her benefit—three times the 'disregard' if she is married. Quite simply, says Murray, 'In the low-skilled working class, marriage makes no sense.'[55]

The Effects on the Children: The National Child Development Study is based on a national sample of children born in 1958. The first major report on the 1958 cohort looked at the children in 1966 when they were aged seven. There have been four further follow-up studies, the latest of which was published in October 1993. The study found that illegitimate children experienced earlier death,[56] suffered more accidents,[57] moved house and consequently changed school more frequently,[58] read less well, had a lower arithmetic age and less general knowledge.

Information from three tests of attainment were used: one tested the children's general mental development; the second, reading ability; and the third 'arithmetic age'. Under the first test, teachers graded each child according to his or her general knowledge. The categories were: 'exceptionally well-informed', 'good background knowledge', 'average', 'below average, rather limited', or 'largely ignorant of the world around it'.[59] The results were reported for three groups of children: adopted children, those born within marriage, and those born outside. Forty-nine per cent of the adopted children were graded 'average', along with 49 per cent of the legitimate children and 47 per cent of the illegitimate. Twenty-eight per cent of the legitimate children were said to be 'below average', but 45 per cent of the children born outside marriage were thus classified. Four per cent of the children born in wedlock were graded 'largely ignorant of the world around them', but more than 8 per cent of the illegitimate children were so classified.

According to the Southgate reading test, 49 per cent of the illegitimate children were 'poor', the lowest grade, compared with 28 per cent of the children born in wedlock.[60]

The studies of arithmetic age showed a similar result. After adjustment for social class and other factors, the illegitimate children were found to have an 'arithmetic age' of five months younger than the legitimate children.[61]

American studies reveal similar findings. Barbara Dafoe Whitehead's article in the April 1993 issue of *The Atlantic Monthly* has now become something of a classic. The summary at the head of the article reads:

> The social-science evidence is in: though it may benefit the adults involved, the dissolution of intact two-parent families is harmful

> to large numbers of children. Moreover ... family diversity in the form of increasing numbers of single-parent and step-parent families does not strengthen the social fabric but, rather, dramatically weakens and undermines society.[62]

One of the most authoritative US studies is based on a huge survey of 60,000 children carried out by the US Department of Health and Human Services in 1988. Some commentators argue that the children of one-parent families experience problems because of poverty, not because of their family structure. The study carried out by the Department of Health and Human Services shows a 'missing father' effect—measured by physical health, academic performance and emotional or behavioural problems—across all income groups. The problems diminish as you go up the income scale, presumably because wealthier parents can buy better services for their children. But even at the highest incomes, purchasing power proves no substitute for a father.[63]

Crime

When Murray published *Losing Ground* in 1984, he reported crime rates in America up to 1980. The general pattern was that violent crime and property crime had been reasonably stable during the 1950s and until the early 1960s. Homicide fell between 1950 and 1964 from 5.3 per 100,000 to 5.1.[64] Then in about 1964, with variations for each type of crime, the take-off began. By 1980 murder had increased by 122 per cent, rape by 287 per cent and robbery by 296 per cent.[65]

Crime in Britain began its rapid rise from the mid-1950s. By 1960 the rate had risen by 700 per 100,000 of the population, to 1,700 per 100,000. As Norman Dennis notes, this meant the increase alone in the short period 1955-60 was greater than the 'total annual rate in each of the years of the two or three previous generations of English people'.[66] In the following five years, when there was exceptionally low unemployment, the rate rose to 2,600 per 100,000. Dennis reminds us that a common explanation at the time was that people were less likely to be well behaved when the money in their pockets diminished the importance of living a prudent life. That is *low* unemployment was to blame for the rise in the crime rate. 'Why', some commentators asked, 'should a young man worry about his reputation, or even his criminal record, when he could walk with ease from one job to another?'[67]

By 1970 the rate of increase had brought the figure to 3,200 per 100,000. In 1980 the rate was 5,100 per 100,000. The rate was 7,300 per 100,000 by 1985—over seven times the rate thirty years before. As Dennis notes, the rate in 1991, 10,000 per 100,000, was ten times what it had been in 1955, and the *increase* in the rate in the year 1990-91 was *twice* the *total* rate for the year 1955.[68]

In 1970 there were 480 armed robberies. By 1990 there were 3,900, and this rose in the following year to 5,300. This was an eleven-fold increase on 1970, and the increase in the single year was three times the total in 1970.[69]

Charles Murray compares British and American rates. Murder in America remains more common, but by 1992 the risk of being burgled in England and Wales was more than double that in the US. Moreover, the violent crime rate increased by 40 per cent, so that the rate in England and Wales in 1992 was the same as that of the United States in 1985.[70]

Despite the stubborn reality of the facts, there are still commentators who claim that drawing attention to them is 'moral panic'. But, with due allowance for the discrepancies between the rates reported to the police and the findings of the British Crime Survey, the facts speak for themselves.

Socialist Criticisms of Welfare

Just as in America, critics of the harmful effects of indiscriminate welfare in Britain have not been confined to the ranks of free marketeers. Magnet's analysis of America is supported by Norman Dennis' discussions of British cultural change in *Families Without Fatherhood* (co-authored with George Erdos) and *Rising Crime and the Dismembered Family*. Dennis does not treat the benefit system as having very much causal significance, but stresses the influence of opinion formers in the media and the education system who have systematically undermined values that constitute the only hope for the mass of people. Criminals were not regarded as anti-social, but celebrated as revolutionary heroes; and men who refused low-paid jobs were seen, not as work shy, but as rightly refusing to bend the knee to capitalist exploiters. With his fellow 'ethical socialist' A.H. Halsey, Dennis criticises left-leaning intellectuals for abandoning the communal values central to socialism. These 'egoistic socialists' have rejected conventional virtues such as self-restraint and commitment to family in favour of self-indulgence.[71]

One of the most devastating recent critiques of the social security system has been put forward by Labour MP Frank Field. Britain's welfare system, he says, is 'broken-backed':

> the number of claims escalates and so, therefore, does the welfare bill. Yet independence is not encouraged. ... Means tests paralyse self-help discourage self-improvement and tax honesty while at the same time rewarding claimants for being either inactive or deceitful.[72]

The main target of his criticism is means-tested benefits, which he says are 'the poison within the body of the welfare state'. Welfare cheating is the result of means-tested welfare combined with the lack of jobs:

> *Means tests penalise all those values which make strong, vibrant, communities.* Those with savings above a certain level do not qualify. Those who try a part-time job lose almost pound for pound from their benefit. Those who do work, or who have put a little money aside for a rainy day, can qualify, but only if they lie. And the second lie is always easier than the first. Thus the practice of deceit is encouraged by the form of welfare provision. The only cumulative impact of such lying and deceit is the further erosion of any sense of pride, respect and self-worth ...[73]

He estimates that over 17 per cent of the population (including dependants and claimants) relied on income support in 1993, some 9.8m people, compared with 2.9m (5.8 per cent) in 1962. Counting only claimants, 1.2m relied on national assistance in 1950, compared with 5.6m who relied on income support in 1993.[74]

If the major means tested benefits, family credit, housing benefit and council tax benefit, are also taken into account the proportion of the population increases substantially. In 1993, about 9.8m heads of households received either income support or one the major means tested benefits. In 1978/79 the figure was between 4.5m and 5m heads of households. Assuming 1.5 dependants per head of household, Field calculates that 'nearly half' of the population receives income support or a major means tested benefit.[75] This is an over estimate, possibly based on double counting, and official calculations suggest that about a quarter of the population received a major means-tested benefit in 1992/93.[76]

Field is also concerned that benefits help to encourage family breakdown:

> We also need to confront the values which are taught by our social security system. No system of welfare can be independent of values. These values need to be brought to the fore. Is it right, for example, that young, never-married mothers, should gain additional income support premiums when few if any voters think that such behaviour is acceptable, let alone rewardable?[77]

David Selbourne is yet another left-leaning writer who has sensed the moral confusion at the heart of state welfare. He finds Britain to be a 'corrupted liberal order', but his objection is directed not only against free marketeers, but equally if not more strongly against egoistic socialist demands for 'dutiless rights':

> On the one hand, dutiless 'mercenary advantage', organised in its own interest and even seeking to command the state, pits itself against the civic order in the name of the free market; on the other, demand for dutiless benefit from the state and the civic order, similarly organised on behalf of ostensible citizens (or 'protected subjects') in their own interest, seeks to transform claims into rights by mere force of numbers.[78]

Amidst the moral confusion Selbourne discovers that:

> the old socialist—once disposed to regard all claims-to-right in a 'capitalist' civic order as a surrender to 'bourgeois' illusion—can now be found in the van of those making the politics of dutiless right central to their cause.

The mere desire, says Selbourne, 'to have a good job, money, housing, private means of transport and so on' is confused with a *right* that such events should occur.[79]

Thus, several writers who identify themselves as on the left are now warning about the harmful effects of collectivised welfare. How do their arguments compare with classical-liberal analyses?

The Welfare Problem and Oakeshott's Three Inseparables

We can now try to bring together the discussion of civil association in Chapter 2, the criticisms of corporate association in Chapter 3 and the special problems of the welfare system discussed earlier in this chapter.

The social security system has come under severe criticism from all points of the political spectrum. The problem is not the mere presence of a social security system, but the particular attitudes associated with it in recent times. Britain has had a safety-net system for centuries and it has not consistently caused family breakdown and diminished work effort, though in the years up to 1834 the subsidisation of wages and the policy of indiscriminate relief applied in some localities did have similar effects to those observable today. The faults were remedied in 1834 and it was not until the 1960s and 1970s that welfare began to do noticeably more harm than good.

We can identify six key attitudes which became increasingly dominant after the Second World War:

1. Behaviourism. Poor people were understood to be the victims of circumstance and the duty of government was to devise programmes to remedy their problem. It was assumed that people react to outside stimuli which can be manipulated to bring about changes in their conduct. Such behaviourism provides a rationale for political paternalism.

The counter view is that we are persons with a character, capable of intelligent choice, self-improvement, living according to ideals, adopting wise habits, and bearing personal responsibility. Problems such as poverty, it follows, can only be understood and solved if we accept that in all situations—including those not entirely of our making—we nonetheless are personally responsible for our subsequent actions and decisions.

2. *Victimism.* Closely allied to the behaviourist approach is victimism. But it goes further. Not only is poverty considered to be the result of external forces, these forces are seen as unjust and the victim entitled to compensation. This view and its defects has been discussed in Chapter 3. Not only does it undermine personal responsibility by telling victims that they are incapable of solving their own problems, it provides a rationale for group hatred and demands for political discrimination.

3. *Non-judgementalism.* This doctrine frequently goes hand in hand with victimism, but is distinct. It derives largely from the belief that no one should be criticised because to do so is 'authoritarian'. To moralise is to impose values on others and no one has any grounds for doing so. This doctrine has been criticised in Chapter 2. Its mistake is to confuse external control with self-imposed moral restraint.

4. *Resource rights.* We all enjoy rights in the form of protections against invasions of our freedom. These protective rights are fundamental to a free society. Indeed, freedom is precisely the ability to act within a legally-protected domain of initiative. Welfare rights are different. They are 'resource rights', or demands that political power be used to take the earnings or savings of one group for transfer to another. They are calls for other people to work or save in order that the holder of the right can live without necessarily working or saving. Protective rights by comparison are intended to give everyone a chance. They imply a sense of solidarity which rests on the inclusion of all persons under the same legal and moral conditions and the corresponding acceptance that we cannot exempt ourselves. Such protective rights are mutual, whereas resource rights are confiscatory. Protective rights apply equally to all and self-exemption is improper. Resource rights encourage self-exemption by assuming that

money will be taken from one set of people for the benefit of another. Such rights divide the community between warring factions.

5. Confusion of relief of poverty with equalisation. Further distortion has resulted from the deliberate confusion of the relief of poverty with redistributive justice. The intention of many public policies has not been primarily to relieve poverty, but to eradicate the material reflections of human differences. This pernicious doctrine has already been criticised in Chapter 3.

6. Integrationism. Citizenship theorists argue that giving people spending power integrates them into the community, and that people are excluded from the community without spending power. As Chapter 3 argued, this notion is based on a materialistic view of the human condition. It assumes the solidarity of corporate association, not the moral commitment of civil association.

Some in the Labour party identified the solidarity they sought with social class—they were fighting the class war on behalf of the workers who were 'getting their own back'. For Titmuss—by far the most influential voice in social policy in the 1950s and 60s—and the non-Marxist left this was not the ruling principle, but rather 'citizenship'. Recipients of benefits were victims who should not be blamed, but embraced within the community—admitted to citizenship—by granting them greater spending capacity.

It may be contrasted with the ethos of the American left which also sought to increase the spending capacity of the poor. But, for them, freedom was power. Consequently, they sought to free themselves from guilt and the poor from their lack of spending power. The American view was, therefore, more individualistic than that of Titmuss, though for its libertarian-collectivist protagonists it had the status of an idealistic faith, which allowed them to believe they were serving others.

Oakeshott's explanatory framework helps us to see more clearly where these doctrines come from and where they are leading. Both the Titmuss 'victim-citizen' and the US 'victim-with-attitude' are viewed by their intellectual champions as weak characters in need of outside assistance from the well-to-do. But the aid is not based on the mutual respect of equal citizens, one of whom is temporarily down on his luck, (described below, p. 127) rather it is more or less permanent one-sided aid. Titmuss deliberately caricatured charity as involving a gratitude imperative, ignoring all the efforts typically made by charities (below p. 127) to avoid falling into that trap.

But what of the citizenship of which some analysts speak? The unity they aspire to is that of role players under guidance. All the main human cares are to be provided for by the authorities and the task of the government is to manage people's lives. Thus, the victim-citizen theory of Titmuss and his modern successors—including self-styled one-nation Tories—is incompatible with liberty in three ways.

First, the community of which it speaks is the solidarity of common purpose under direction, not the solidarity of shared acceptance of rules from which no one may exempt himself. The solidarity of civil association is a unity of mutually respecting persons.

Second, it rests on a view of government as paternalistic supervisor, not confined to the important but limited task of maintaining the rules of justice in good shape and providing strictly limited public services.

And third, it is based on a low view of human potential. Two types of harm result, according to writers like J.S. Mill and Tocqueville. Undermining personal responsibility is bad for individuals because it reduces the quality of their lives. Schemes to assist the less fortunate should appeal to the best in the beneficiaries, by discovering their strengths and not enhancing their weaknesses, thus raising their horizons and potential for self-improvement.

No less important, relieving people of personal responsibility threatens liberty. Democracy rests on citizens who are genuinely independent of government and not its creatures. And a truly independent public opinion, able to check corruption or excess in government, assumes a nation made up of strong, educated and responsible characters. The mainspring of a free and democratic society is the individual's sense of personal responsibility, and any system that erodes it endangers liberty by rendering people less able to play their part as free citizens, both in the workplace and the democratic process. As J.S. Mill wrote, formal instruction is only one of the means of learning. Almost as indispensable is a 'vigorous exercise of the active energies' involving judgement and self-control. These energies are stimulated by the 'difficulties of life' and to remove them out of misplaced sympathy would be dangerous because:

> A people among whom there is no habit of spontaneous action for a collective interest—who look habitually to their government to command or prompt them in all matters of joint concern—who expect to have everything done for them, except what can be made an affair of mere habit and routine—have their faculties only half developed.[80]

Such a system, says Mill, promotes despotism, 'by arming with intellectual superiority as an additional weapon those who already have the legal power'. The only safeguard against political slavery is 'the check maintained over governors by the diffusion of intelligence, activity and public spirit among the governed.' And for this reason all sections of society should have 'much to do for themselves' and, as far as possible, manage their joint concerns by voluntary co-operation.[81]

To sum up: there is a degree of acceptance among critics of otherwise varying points of view that the problem of welfare is moral in nature. It is having harmful effects on human character, encouraging the breakdown of the family, crowding out the voluntary associations on which the moral order of a free society rests and, as if these were not serious enough, it also fails to accomplish its chief declared aim of reducing poverty.

5

Making a Reality of Civil Association

IN THIS chapter I attempt to state more positively some of the measures that are necessary today to create a society of civil associates. The chapter tries to improve upon the argument first published in the final part of *Reinventing Civil Society*. Because a shorthand label is useful, I will call the whole body of ideas civic capitalism.

The measures required to make a reality of civil association can be placed in three groups. They involve both public policy measures and private action plans.

First, we need a clear view about law and the importance of de-politicising it. This will involve confining the state to its proper task of maintaining the conditions on which liberty rests and it will require acknowledgement of a higher constitutional law setting out binding principles which limit what governments may do.

Second, we need to restore a sense of personal responsibility and to rehabilitate virtue in its best sense, without puritanism. We need to revive confidence in the view of the human condition which sees human nature as suited to a life of reflection, choice, and mutually respectful habits—a view badly damaged by twentieth century collectivism.

Third, we need a positive campaign to restore tasks to civil society, that is to the domain of 'community without politics'. This objective goes hand in hand with the second aim. There can be no virtue without practice and no practice while the state monopolises all important services. A good deal of what is proposed requires co-ordinated private action. Governments should step back to create the space for a renewal of public but not political action; and second, they should refrain from actions which undermine personal responsibility, the family and voluntary associations. The rest is up to us.

De-Politicising the Law-Making Process

My main task is to propose how to reform the welfare state, but there is one general problem which is so fundamental that it cannot be neglected. I will, however, only touch upon it briefly.

One of the most urgent challenges is to refresh our understanding of the ideal of liberty under law. Early classical liberals put their faith in the separation of powers—legislative, judicial and executive. However, the separation was never fully achieved, even in America which entrenched the separation of powers in a written constitution. Power was divided between the federal government and the states, in addition to the separation of federal powers, but it failed to contain the growth of central power because law-making was not sufficiently separated from policy-making. The Supreme Court was intended to check the politicisation of law-making but it too became politicised.

According to Hayek, classical-liberal thinkers have been insufficiently on their guard against the perversion of the law-making process by politics. Consequently, we urgently need to renew efforts to put the law above government. This will mean distinguishing between three types of law. First, constitutional law, governing the powers of government and what it may do and how it may proceed. Second, laws which are intended to protect the liberty of individuals, that is to mark out a domain of initiative by stating the rules that must be obeyed on pain of punishment. Third, laws which are little more than administrative commands to public servants to carry out the tasks of government. Laws understood as 'rules of just conduct', as Hayek called them, are the means to liberty. Laws as administrative commands are the instrumental means to the government's ends. Rules of just conduct leave ends to individuals in voluntary association; administrative commands tell individuals what to do. Any such change is, of course, made more difficult by Britain's membership of the European Union—yet another reason for doubting the value of any pan-European federation.

Most law in the seventeenth and eighteenth centuries was common law. Judges or scholars discovered it, they did not make it. The idea that the law was above interference by mere governments derived in part from the much earlier view that the law was God's law. William Blackstone, for instance, whose *Commentaries on the Laws of England* became the most influential legal guide on both sides of the Atlantic, believed that law was based on the will of God, who had provided us with two kinds of law: 'revealed law' and the 'law of nature'. Revealed law, as expressed in the scriptures, was of 'infinitely more authority' because it was 'expressly declared so to be by God himself', whereas the law of nature was 'only what, by the assistance of human reason, we imagine that law to be'. The laws of individual nations or localities depended on natural and revealed law. No human law, he says, 'should be suffered to contradict them'.[1]

In keeping with Blackstone's view, it was taken for granted that no mere person or mere government could alter God's law. Similarly, no mere government could be allowed to interfere with law because it was the very means of limiting the capacity of rulers to abuse their powers. The intention was to prevent the law from becoming either the instrument of special interests, or the mere tool of government. It must be that body of moral and prudential rules which is binding on everyone.

The purpose of law as a servant of liberty, said Blackstone, was to ensure:

> that every man may know what to look upon as his own, what as another's; what absolute and what relative duties are required at his hands; what is to be esteemed honest, dishonest, or indifferent; what degree every man retains of his natural liberty; what he has given up as the price of the benefits of society; and after what manner each person is to moderate the use and exercise of those rights which the state assigns him, in order to promote and secure the public tranquillity.[2]

To restore confidence in impartial law two tasks are necessary. First, we should stop thinking of law as the instrument of factions or political parties for achieving their aims. The law should be above parties. And second, to effect the distinction between 'instrumental law' and 'moral law' or 'commands' and 'law' we should establish two separate chambers. Hume has described how a distinction was drawn in the seventeenth century between 'laws' which were permanent and 'proclamations' which lasted only during the king's reign.[3] Hayek later captured this distinction by differentiating between 'rules of just conduct' and 'commands'. Just as proclamations had force during the King's life only, so modern party-political commands should be of limited duration. Law in the proper sense should be made by a separate chamber, in a separate process and require more than a bare majority. As Blackstone put it, law is above all a rule: 'not a transient sudden order from a superior to or concerning a particular person; but something permanent, uniform and universal'.[4]

Most law today is enacted by parliaments to achieve particular purposes. The idea of law as a 'rule of just conduct' is barely understood. To retrieve it will take a long time and is very unlikely to be accomplished while law makers are party politicians who hope to gain power by offering financial gains to a majority of the voters. US republicans have (unsuccessfully) proposed term limitations to create citizen legislators. This measure would have been a small step in the right direction, but it alone cannot achieve its intended purpose. The ultimate aim must be to secure the election of a legislature returned to office without having promised to deliver material benefits to one group or another.

Hayek proposed that the making of the 'rules of just conduct' should be the task of a separate assembly and argued that historically Britain's mistake was to have allowed the same assembly that voted taxes also to make laws. Law-making is too important to be so determined. It requires a different temper, an impartial spirit, and a degree of wisdom, of which no party political debating chamber is capable. In order to separate the promulgation of decrees dealing with particular matters from the making of rules of just conduct,

Hayek suggested the establishment of *two* elected popular assemblies: one charged with governing in the sense of carrying out a party programme, and the other charged with enacting the *nomos* or universal laws. He believed that people would choose very different representatives for the two assemblies, for effectiveness in upholding justice demands 'probity, wisdom, and judgement', qualities displayed by few of today's party politicians.[5]

Restoring Personal Responsibility

As *Reinventing Civil Society* emphasised, earlier champions of liberty took it for granted that we should seek to serve higher ideals. Work, for instance, at its best was seen as a vocation. It was not a mere necessity for making ends meet, but a duty to be undertaken for the greater good and in the right spirit of mutual respect. Outside the workplace there was an obligation to 'do your bit' by supporting voluntary associations and primary groups central to communal life. They included churches, charities for assisting the less fortunate, friendly societies for mutual aid and, above all, the family.

The ideal of liberty extends far beyond the commercial sector of the economy. Historically its supporters wanted to create and foster institutions that would encourage self-improvement. Civic capitalists always understood that life is a perpetual struggle against imperfection. They did not, of course, expect perfection to be achieved. They saw moral improvement as a strictly voluntary process: to force people to be better was a contradiction in terms, for to be a better person was precisely to improve despite pressures to the contrary.

This guiding ethos is well captured in Samuel Smiles' books on *Self-Help, Character, Thrift* and *Duty*. This, for instance, is how Smiles spoke of character. There are many persons, he said, who have no other possession in the world but their character, 'and yet they stand as firmly upon it as any crowned king'.[6] Accomplishment was a separate matter:

> A man may be accomplished in art, literature, and science, and yet, in honesty, virtue, truthfulness, and the spirit of duty, be entitled to take rank after many a poor and illiterate peasant.[7]

And a person's wealth was of little consequence. Smiles' appeal was to everyone, rich or poor:

> Still less has wealth any necessary connection with elevation of character. On the contrary, it is much more frequently the cause of its corruption and degradation. Wealth and corruption, luxury and vice, have very close affinities to each other. Wealth, in the hands of men of weak purpose, of deficient self-control, or of ill-regulated passions, is only a temptation and a snare—the source, it may be, of infinite mischief both to themselves and to others.[8]

When Smiles spoke of self-help he did not mean selfishness. In the 1866 edition of his book he said in the Preface that the title of the book had proved 'unfortunate' because it had led some 'to suppose that it consists of a eulogy of selfishness'. This was the 'very opposite' of what he had intended. The duty of 'helping one's self in the highest sense', he insisted, involves the helping of one's neighbours'. Today, the libertarian collectivists described by Magnet and Dennis are inclined to mock any talk of virtue.

Gertrude Himmelfarb has argued that the Victorians spoke of 'virtues' and not 'values' for good reason, because 'virtues' imply clear rules of conduct whereas 'values' imply mere opinion or preference. Libertarian collectivists invariably use the term virtue to speak of sexual chastity, and then proceed to caricature the Victorian view as concerned with obsessive trivialities like the clothing of 'naked' piano legs.[9] The typical Victorian was only too aware that a concern with 'full-frontal' piano legs had little connection with real virtue.

Historically, the champions of freedom were also the champions of virtue and, as Chapter 2 argued, we have been misled by libertarian moral relativism to suspect all calls for virtue as demands for authoritarianism. But as Burke understood:

> Men are qualified for civil liberty in exact proportion to their disposition to put moral chains upon their own appetites; in

> proportion as their love to justice is above their rapacity; in proportion as their soundness and sobriety of understanding is above their vanity and presumption; in proportion as they are more disposed to listen to the counsels of the wise and good, in preference to the flattery of knaves. Society cannot exist unless a controlling power upon will and appetite be placed somewhere, and the less of it there is within, the more there must be without. It is ordained in the eternal constitution of things, that men of intemperate minds cannot be free. Their passions forge their fetters.[10]

Champions of liberty should also be champions of duty, that is, the sense of personal responsibility which enjoins us to make the world a better place and to give generously of our own time and energy in the service of others. But, if liberty rests on virtue and if virtue is primarily moulded in the family, as Adam Smith believed (above p. 11), should champions of liberty bolster traditional family life? And should they expect the state to play its part in sustaining the family? Liberty rests on some institutions, habits, values and dispositions being seen as sacrosanct. Some free marketeers and many on the left would mock any such claim but, as Frank Knight argued, classical liberalism has always had its sacred, untouchable elements. Private property was the foremost, but in common with Hayek, Knight did not shrink from putting the family in the same category.[11] He went so far as to say that liberalism, in a sense 'never really meant individualism'. Each person, he says:

> comes into the world destitute and helpless, and necessarily remains a liability for a large fraction of his life-span, before he can become an asset to himself or an 'individual' with capacity for membership in an organisation of responsible units. In the nature of the case, liberalism is more 'familism' than literal individualism.

And Knight, who was a severe critic of over-mighty government, believed that public policy should protect the family. No society, according to Knight, could possibly hope to flourish without primary groups like the family and to safeguard them where necessary, 'must be the first concern of any intelligent social policy—on a level with the preservation of physical life itself'.

Adam Smith, too, did not believe that the law should be silent on the family. The law should for the most part prohibit injury but it can, and should, go further:

> The laws of all civilized nations oblige parents to maintain their children, and children to maintain their parents, and impose upon men many other duties of beneficence. The civil magistrate is entrusted with the power not only of preserving the public peace by restraining injustice, but of promoting the prosperity of the commonwealth, by establishing good discipline, and by discouraging every sort of vice and impropriety; he may prescribe rules, therefore, which not only prohibit mutual injuries among fellow-citizens, but command mutual good offices to a certain degree.[12]

Smith also saw that it was potentially dangerous for laws to require the fulfilment of duties of benevolence. To neglect the task would expose the society 'to many gross disorders and shocking enormities', but to go too far might be 'destructive of all liberty, security, and justice'. But he did not conclude that the government should refrain from such regulation. On the contrary, he believed it was vital to make the effort to get the balance right. Law, for instance, was important in encouraging the best in family life. If divorce was too easy, he argued, it tended to undermine trust between the couple, because both were 'continually in fear of being dismissed by the other party'.[13] He accepted that divorce law could be too strict, but thought it better that the knot was 'too strait' than too loose.[14] The law had also played an important role in making the relationship between men and women in marriage more equal, a development of which he approved.

Refashioning a Public-but-not-Political Domain

One of the priorities of public policy should be to restore functions to civil society. We need a movement which takes pride in ensuring that vital tasks are undertaken without resort to government. Is this ambition realistic?

Fortunately, we have an admirable but neglected historical tradition on which to build. During the eighteenth and nineteenth centuries the prevailing ethos of the friendly societies and charities was to take personal pride in assuming responsibility for the direct resolution of problems. Today, few take this view, yet for much of the history of Britain and the US free citizens were only too keen to establish committees or organisations to tackle the issues of the day. This activism is still a part of the Western make-up, but today it is more likely to lead to demands that the government—which means *other* people—takes action. The churches were once central to encouraging private philanthropy, but today they too are more likely to demand action by the state. They are also likely to define the good citizen as the one who demands state measures with the greatest vehemence, a doctrine which is the very opposite of the spirit of philanthropy consistent with liberty. It is doubly pernicious because, on one hand, it denies personal responsibility, and on the other, it dresses up political demands as altruism when they are no such thing.

The restoration of civil society will require measures to return much of the welfare state, including health, education and pension provision to its rightful owners, the people. These services will be the subject of separate studies, and in this publication I concentrate on the hardest challenge of all, the case for private relief of poverty.

Many can accept the case for wider choice in health, education and pensions, but believe that the relief of poverty is entirely a matter for government. Today's adult generations have grown up under the welfare state, and whatever doubts may be entertained about its harmful side-effects, the majority of people cannot envisage any alternative. Collectivists have successfully implanted the doctrine that welfare is a state responsibility, and that private welfare has only a subordinate or residual role, especially in the relief of poverty.

Should we take private welfare seriously? Could it be an alternative to the welfare state? Has it not already been tried and failed? Isn't that why the welfare state was introduced in the first place?

What is the state's responsibility for the poor? It goes without saying that no one should be allowed to starve or suffer severe privation, a view which has been accepted by nations in the British tradition since the middle ages. The presence of a safety net should not be left to chance and the public authorities are well placed to ensure that no one falls through it.

But, if it is a legitimate responsibility of the state to prevent people falling below a certain income threshold, then no government can also escape considering how best to maintain this safety net without doing more harm than good. And here lies the problem. It has in practice proved to be very difficult to provide a minimum without also producing harmful side effects. J.S. Mill has stated the problem as well as anyone:

> in all cases of helping, there are two sets of consequences to be considered; the *consequences of the assistance itself*, and the consequences of *relying* on the assistance. The former are generally beneficial, but the latter, for the most part, injurious; so much so, in many cases, as greatly to outweigh the value of the benefit.[15]

This is never more likely to happen, he thought, than in the very cases where the need for help is the most intense. However, Mill also saw that help for those 'paralysed by discouragement' could serve as a tonic and not a sedative. Such help was bracing, so long as it did not discourage self-help. He recommended the general maxim:

> that if assistance is given in such a manner that the condition of the person helped is as desirable as that of the person who succeeds in doing the same thing without help, the assistance, if capable of being previously calculated on, is mischievous: but if, while available to everybody, it leaves to every one a strong motive to do without it if he can, it is then for the most part beneficial.[16]

In other words, if assistance made individuals better off than if they worked and they were able to rely on the cash payments being continued, independence would be undermined. Consequently, the state should provide a bare minimum guarantee for all, and reserve for private judgment 'the task of distinguishing between one case of real necessity and another'. Public officials, Mill said, will not 'take the trouble of ascertaining and sifting the past conduct of a person in distress, so as to form a rational judgement on it'. Private charity can make these distinctions and is entitled to do so because it is spending its own money, but officials administering public funds should not be required to provide more than the minimum. If they were, 'indulgence very speedily becomes the rule, and refusal the more or less capricious or tyrannical exception'.[17] The dominant view for much of this century has been that people are poor because they have been affected by factors outside their control. The distinctive feature of Mill's approach is that it treats poor people as moral agents, not as victims of circumstance. Moreover, he anticipates a much bigger role for private philanthropy.

The modern doctrine of welfare rights seems at first sight to be based on respect for individuals: our common humanity, so the argument goes, demands that we all enjoy equal rights. But in truth the demand for welfare rights removes the relationship between giver and receiver from the moral domain. It *de*-moralizes the relationship.[18]

Social policy analysts have typically argued that any charitable help always involves 'stigma', and that the only way to eliminate the stigma is to make payments by right.[19] Their assumption seems to be that all *voluntary* help entails stigma: that the very act of giving by choice involves a slight. First, giving help does not necessarily imply disrespect, though help *may* be given in a manner which belittles the receiver. It does not follow, therefore, that we should abandon voluntary help. Instead, we should take great pains to give help in the right spirit. The only real way of avoiding disrespect is to ensure reciprocity between giver and receiver. I will elaborate in a moment.

Second, to demand help by right is to demand that force be applied to other people. But this use of compulsion strips the relationship of reciprocity, the only true basis for mutual respect. We should aim, therefore, to base a policy of assisting the less fortunate, not on 'rights', which are demands that other people be compelled to render assistance, but on duties, which reach within us all for our better nature.

But does the record of private philanthropy suggest that it is capable of assuming responsibility for assistance of the poor? Let me concentrate on two questions. First, how the beneficiaries of nineteenth-century charity were seen, and especially whether they were classified into the 'deserving' and 'undeserving'. And second, what were the relative responsibilities of the individual, the community and the state?

The Changing Perception of Poverty

During the eighteenth century and until the end of the nineteenth, philanthropists in the tradition of Sir Frederick Eden (whose classic study, *The State of the Poor*, was published in 1796) focused on 'the poor', a term which implied that the poor were always with us. However, by the time Charles Booth published *Life and Labour of the People in London* between 1891 and 1903, the emphasis had shifted to 'poverty', a term which implied that the condition could be eradicated. However, it also implied that the condition to be eradicated was a lack of money, an assumption questioned by some contemporary observers.

C.S. Loch, for instance, the secretary of the Charity Organisation Society (COS) from 1875 to 1914, argued that to speak of poverty in the manner of Booth and Rowntree (who studied poverty in York in 1899) was to see the problem as one of money alone, and the public policy issue as how best to get additional money to some people. But the real problem was not money but 'social habit'. People of similar means, Loch said, do not live in the same way and if some were poor the real challenge was to discover what could be changed in their circumstances or lifestyle in order to restore their independence.[20]

Loch had two main objections to the assumption of responsibility for maintenance by the state. First, it excluded the ethical dimension because, by defining the problem as one of money transfer, it failed to do justice to human nature, and especially to man's moral nature. Second, it excluded the motives of 'energy and endeavour' that spring from personal responsibility. Indiscriminate relief 'attracts the applicant by an appeal to his weakness, and it requires of him no effort'. He preferred to appeal to the strength of the applicant.[21] Loch's criticism was, therefore, not purely economic. His focus was not on the perverse incentives of welfare, though that was part of it. He saw society as far more than an incentive system. Charity, he said, appeals to personal duty and thought.[22] It is thought, the process of acting intelligently, justly, courageously and more, that gives man dignity.

By the 1960s these arguments had been forgotten and the de-moralizing of the less fortunate had gone further still. Campaigners preferred to speak of 'relative' poverty, a doctrine presented as progressive whereas, in reality, it was more akin to the old view that 'the poor' are always with us, for it defined poverty so that some percentage of the population is always poor. A common method is to treat those with less than 50 per cent of the average (or median) wage as poor, thus entrenching dependency. No less important, its protagonists have got away with presenting anyone who criticises their view as inhumane, whereas the counter-emphasis, represented at the turn of the century by C.S. Loch and today by writers like Charles Murray, is on finding ways for everyone to escape poverty by becoming as independent as possible. The relativists, however, want and anticipate a permanently dependent population, just as the aristocrats of old did.

The Charity Organisation Society is often presented as having been too quick to distinguish between the deserving and the undeserving poor. Gertrude Himmelfarb, in a re-appraisal of the evidence, argues that the spirit that moved the reformers in the last quarter of the 19th century and up to World War One was the desire to assist the labouring poor. The COS did not regard poverty as entirely a function of character. On the contrary, it recognized the 'causeless', 'exceptional', and 'temporary' nature of a good deal of poverty.[23] But, in any event, as early as the mid-1880s the term 'undeserving' had fallen out of favour. In 1886 it was altered (in the COS reports although not in the case studies) to read 'not likely to benefit', and two years later to the still more neutral 'not assisted'. By 1905 the revised edition of the COS's *Principles of Decision* officially abandoned the criterion of 'deserving', preferring: 'The test is not whether the applicant is deserving but whether he is helpable.'[24] C.S. Loch put it this way. The problem, he said:

> is not whether the person is 'deserving' or 'undeserving', but whether, granted the facts, the distress can be stayed and self-support attained. If the help can be given privately from within the circle of the family, so much the better. Sometimes it may be best to advise, but not to interfere. In some cases but little help may be necessary; in others again the friendly relation between applicant and friend may last for months and even years.[25]

The reputation of the Charity Organisation Society (COS) has suffered from many caricatures at the hands of socialist intellectuals. In practice the attitude it encouraged was exemplary. Helen Bosanquet, one of its leading lights, hauled one lady bountiful over the coals for fearing that poverty might be 'cured', for if it were, the lady had argued, 'the rich would have no one upon whom to exercise their faculty of benevolence'; and Mrs Bosanquet lambasted another who objected to giving the poor the means of self-sufficiency because that would make them too independent. Without this 'glow of benevolent patronage', she commented, 'the ladies bountiful of this world would soon lose their interest in the poor'.[26]

The COS believed that the ideal to aim for was mutual respect between giver and taker: no presumption of superiority by the giver, and no doffing of caps by the receiver. This spirit is captured by an incident in Dickens' *Hard Times* when Stephen Blackpool, an honest and hard-working power-loom weaver in Josiah Bounderby's factory, is unfairly sacked. His plight is desperate, for he has no money and no chance of other work in the locality without a reference from Bounderby. He faces a long and arduous journey by foot in search of employment. Bounderby's wife, who believes her husband was unjust, offers Stephen a bank note to see him through the hard times ahead. He takes only £2, a much smaller sum than she offered because, he says, he knows he can pay that much back.[27] In other words, despite his dire predicament, he will not allow the relationship to be one-sided and will accept only a loan. Mutual respect between giver and receiver was maintained.

The giving of help is undoubtedly difficult to accomplish without demeaning the recipient, and during the last century great effort was expended to discover and encourage the right approach. The charities of that time issued their employees and volunteers with guidelines or manuals to instil mutual respect. Selections from some of these guidelines have been reproduced in an excellent study of philanthropy by F.K. Prochaska:

> Remember, it is a 'privilege' not a 'right' to enter the poor man's cottage. Be sympathetic, not patronizing. Be a friend, not a relieving lady. Avoid giving money. Do not promote a spirit of dependence. Distinguish cases of real misery from those of fictitious distress. Avoid favouritism. Be an expert on domestic management. Quote the Scriptures. Avoid religious controversy. Encourage school attendance. Avoid politics. Show that almsgiving is not merely the duty of the rich, but also the privilege of the poor. Be regular in your visits.[28]

One of the primary aims of reformers was to improve character. Today, to make any such claim would be criticised as patronising or authoritarian. Modern social policy analysts typically consider it inhumane to criticise or blame an individual who is experiencing hardship due to his own conduct. The humane approach is assumed to be giving money, and anything else is caricatured as making excuses for *not* giving money. But can it legitimately be claimed that to pass judgement on a person's conduct is automatically uncaring or inhumane?

Consider the opposite of blame, praise. When we praise someone we applaud their accomplishment in the hope of encouraging still greater effort and achievement. Is blame not similar? We blame or criticise in order to encourage people to do better next time. The social-policy mainstream is preoccupied with 'stigma', which originally meant a mark branded on a slave or criminal. To avoid stigmatising someone appears at first sight to be humane because it would be wrong to stain a person's character permanently. But if we criticise a person who has fallen on hard times due to his own inappropriate behaviour, we do not brand him a permanent failure. We offer criticism because we believe him capable of more. Failure is not a permanent state. Indeed it is vital to human growth, for it is through our failures as well as our successes that we develop our personalities. To criticise a person is to treat him as a dignified individual capable of inner growth.

It is sometimes said today that free marketeers want to leave problems 'where they lie', as if they are concerned only to find excuses for inaction. That there should always be help available, even for those who are unequivocally to blame, goes without saying. Even the gambler, drug addict or drunk should be helped. But it is *how* we help that matters. At the end of the last century the desirability of good character was not so much at issue between socialists and individualists, as modern historians Gertrude Himmelfarb, Brian Harrison and Stefan Collini, as well as nineteenth-century observers, have noted. The ludicrous claim that to assign personal responsibility is 'blaming the victim', described in Chapter 3, found no serious nineteenth century adherents at any point of the political spectrum.

The key word in economics in the 1890s, according to one socialist quoted by both Collini and Himmelfarb, was 'character'. According to the *Encyclopaedia of Social Reform*, the reason why 'individualist economists fear socialism is that they believe it will deteriorate character, and the reason why socialist economists seek socialism is their belief that under individualism character is deteriorating'.[29] Fabian socialists, for instance, believed that their system would produce 'a higher type of character' and Alfred Marshall, the leading economist of his day, called for 'chivalry' and, in the opening pages of his *Principles of Economics*, stressed the centrality of character to the study of economics.[30]

The Individual, the Community and the State

The dominant view during the nineteenth century was not that all problems were individual, but rather that a combination of effort by the individual, the community and the state was required. But when observers emphasised that there must be a common effort, they did not only mean that the government must do something. There was a strong sense of community responsibility which was distinguished from the state.

One of the intentions of the COS was to create social solidarity. It believed that the 'social' aspect of visiting, even more than the charitable, was the means by which 'class distinctions may be partly effaced'. Hence the COS urged its visitors to be friendly and 'neighbourly', to give charity not as 'from strangers to strangers' but as a 'transaction between people personally known to each other'. Only in such a personal relationship would the rich appreciate 'the responsibility attaching to wealth and leisure' and the poor have 'the comfortable assurance that if the day of exceptional adversity should come, they will not be left to encounter it without a friend'.[31]

But charities in the COS tradition were not blind to the role of the state. They also sought political reform. According to Loch, the duty of charity was to seek both to intensify the sense of membership of society and also to improve social conditions through legal reform.[32] Shaftesbury, for example, had earlier pushed through the factory acts, while others urged prison reform, child protection laws, housing reform, and much more. But the COS did not, as Loch put it, aim at 'recasting society itself on a new non-economic plan', as did socialism.[33]

For C.S. Loch and his associates, welfare in a free society meant that primary responsibility lay with the individual and his family, but also that no one should be left to cope alone. The community in the form of voluntary associations should always be there to help and the state should be in the background, ready to assist but within proper limits.

There were two elements of this philanthropic ethos. First, there was 'community without politics', a sense of solidarity with others that is based on an obligation to help each other without degrading the recipient. The contrast is not between community and individualism, but between rival types of community. A 'moral community' respects the diverse purposes that may be pursued by individuals each acting under accepted legal and moral limits, and the aim of any assistance is to restore individuals to membership of the moral community. A 'political community' assumes that lives are to be directed by the authorities and, because it is based on low expectations, tends to lock into their predicament people who are temporarily down on their luck.

And second, there was a sense of 'duty without rights'. Everyone, and especially the wealthy, had a duty to help but no one had a right to receive it. Giver and receiver were both expected to take pains to show mutual respect.

This ethos was more than pious hope. The extent of charitable effort was huge. The leading historians of philanthropy have not been able to gauge its full extent, since it was spontaneous and dispersed. A recent study by Geoffrey Finlayson quotes a contemporary estimate which put the annual expenditure of private charities in London in 1870 at between £5.5m and £7m, when London contained about ten per cent of the population.[34] If total charitable giving in England and Wales is put at £55m, it dwarfs the total expenditure on poor relief in England and Wales of £8m in 1871.

The scale of charity was enormous, but it affected far fewer people than mutual aid.[35] Over three quarters of those covered by the 1911 National Insurance Act were already members of friendly societies: 9.5m out of 12m.

Mutual aid associations sharply contrasted themselves with charities. Charity was one set of people helping another set;

mutual aid was putting money aside in a common fund and helping each other when the need arose. As one leading society put it, the benefits were rights:

> For certain benefits in sickness ... [we] subscribe to one fund. That fund is our Bank; and to draw therefrom is the independent and manly right of every Member, whenever the contingency for which the funds are subscribed may arise, as freely as if the fund was in the hand of their own banker, and they had but to issue a cheque for the amount. These are not BENEVOLENCES —they are rights.[36]

This language of rights was later purloined by the welfare state to mean something very different.

The friendly societies, as well as the charities, took responsibility for helping people to avoid resort to the poor law. For instance, arguing against proposals for a British compulsory state pension scheme in 1882, a spokesman for the 600,000-strong Ancient Order of Foresters friendly society pointed out that thrift had succeeded in considerably reducing the number of paupers. The increased facilities for thrift 'afforded to the British Workman by his own peculiar organisations', friendly societies and trade unions, had done much during the previous thirty years to reduce pauperism, he said. They could look forward to the time when pauperism would be reduced to those suffering from 'insanity and contagion' and he pointed with pride to the reduction in pauperism since 1849. In that year paupers had comprised 6.2 per cent of the population of England; in 1859, 4.4 per cent; in 1869, 4.7 per cent; and in 1879, only 3.0 per cent.[37]

Friendly society members included those very workers whose incomes were just sufficient to keep poverty at bay. In his evidence to the Royal Commission on the Poor Laws of 1909, J.L. Stead, the permanent secretary of the Foresters, expressed his pride in the fact that his society had low-paid members: 'We have got some of the humblest men in the country in our society, and we are just as proud of them as of the others.'[38]

Thus, mutual insurance prevented many an employee from having to resort, not only to the poor law, but also to charity. As a result, the downward trend in reliance on the poor law continued until the eve of World War One. In 1892 the figure was still lower at 2.6 per cent and in 1908, 2.2 per cent.[39]

A fuller discussion of the role of friendly societies can be found in *Reinventing Civil Society*, but the common element to the services provided by friendly societies was independence. They provided all the services which enabled people to be self-supporting. The great fear was that illness would prevent self support. Consequently, the friendly societies provided a benefit if the breadwinner fell ill or was injured. Medical expenses when ill were also covered. Medical care when ill was available. Usually doctors were paid a capitation fee in return for free care, but the societies also organised medical institutes where service was provided by salaried medical officers.

More serious still, what would happen if the breadwinner died? The society ensured that widow and orphans were provided for. As age took its toll, independence might also be threatened, and so the societies provided support in old age, although the ethos was different. The usual attitude was to keep working as long as possible with the fall-back of sick pay. If a man lost his job, assistance in the form of travelling benefit was provided. The friendly societies did not provide cash unemployment benefit as such, but rather assistance in finding a new job. Cases of special hardship were met from a special benevolent fund. Thus, every member and his family was covered against the main dangers to independence: illness or injury, death, old-age and loss of job.

The Value of Diversity

One other valuable lesson of nineteenth century experience deserves emphasis. Charities did not always hit upon better ways of doing things. Many also made mistakes, but this too was valuable. One of the most important lessons of history is that there is no perfection in human affairs. The human condition is to struggle for improvement and, once we have learnt valuable lessons, to struggle again to avoid forgetting them. We never know what the future holds, and for this reason we should make arrangements which speed up the process by which we learn from experience. Public sector monopoly acts on the exactly contrary principle. It assumes there is one obvious right answer and that the state can achieve the desired outcome most effectively. The history of welfare teaches us the folly of any such assumption.

For instance, during the second half of the nineteenth century there was a vigorous debate between the 'dole charities', that confined themselves to giving out cash, and the friendly-visiting charities, that emphasised the importance of personal support and strengthening character. People were urged to give practical help rather than mere cash, or to support charities which offered personal support. This argument was played out during the nineteenth century between protagonists in language strikingly reminiscent of today's debates about welfare dependency.

My argument is not that in a competitive system the right answer is always arrived at. It is that by allowing many people to bring about improvements as they believe best and at their own risk, we arrive sooner at the right answers. We learn from the successes and failures of others. However, during the twentieth century when British governments steadily assumed increased responsibility for the poor from the 1911 National Insurance Act onwards, they adopted the dole charity model. It has proved far more difficult to correct that error than it did during the nineteenth century when critics could more readily put their ideas to the test of experience. The COS did not have to fight a political campaign but could proceed by example. As in so many things, the concentration of power has proved to be the enemy of welfare.

The Ethos of Community Without Politics

The ethos which prevailed before the welfare state, may be summarised as follows. From medieval times it was accepted that the state (in the form of the parish authorities) had an obligation to prevent starvation. It is common to date the poor law from the Elizabethan legislation of 1601, but as the Royal Commission on the Poor Laws of 1909 found, the obligation to assist the poor has common-law origins predating the Norman Conquest. By the early fourteenth century, 200 years before the earliest Tudor legislation, the tradition of parish relief was well established.[40] It was possible for a parish officer who allowed an individual to starve in his locality to be prosecuted for manslaughter. It is significant that this requirement was a *duty* placed on the poor law authorities. A duty naturally implies a *right* to assistance, but it had a different effect from a modern *welfare right*, not least because conditions were always attached to receipt of support. In particular, the able-bodied were always expected to perform some work.

Above all, it was also considered something of a disgrace to resort to the parish, and consequently private philanthropy took responsibility for protecting people from having to turn to the poor law. In addition, there were many whose low income put them in danger of having to rely on either the poor law or charity, who took steps to avoid both. They formed mutual aid associations to allow them to create a shared fund on which they could draw in hard times.

Could this model serve as a basis for modern reform? It is obviously utopian in the short run. But I believe it is the ideal to keep in mind as we confront the manifest failings of state welfare.

Public policy should seek to foster a renewal of this three-part ethos of organised welfare: (1) a certain safety net as the minimum, maintained by government; (2) above the safety net a public but not political domain achieved by people assuming responsibility for their less fortunate fellows in a spirit of mutual respect; and (3) a tradition of mutual aid for those who intended to avoid resort not only to the state but also to charity. All this was in addition to the informal assistance of family, neighbours and friends, not to mention commercial insurance.

Chapter 6 asks how we could encourage the re-emergence of this ethos.

6

Some Policy Proposals

THE measures necessary to assist the poor can be summarised under four headings. First, economic growth is necessary. The focus on individual conduct and morals is indispensable to success, but on its own will not be sufficient. Beveridge, in his study of voluntary action, cited William Akroyd speaking at a gathering of poor law guardians in 1841: 'Before it is just to say that a man ought to be an independent labourer, the country ought to be in such a state that a labourer by honest industry can become independent'.[1]

Economic growth is a necessary, but not a sufficient, precondition for the creation of opportunities to escape from poverty. Economic growth depends in large measure on the energy and ingenuity of private citizens, but unwise fiscal and monetary policies can all too easily cancel out human endeavour. Government, therefore, has a responsibility to create an economic framework consistent with liberty. Some unemployment is seasonal, some is due to the trade cycle, and some due to long-term structural changes in economic conditions, but governments can also make unemployment much worse by their actions. Since the Second World War, the failure to control inflation has caused unemployment, as did the return to the gold standard at pre-war parities in 1925, and the more recent tying of the pound to the deutschmark in the Exchange Rate Mechanism.

Second, we should acknowledge that people who are poor due to self-damaging conduct will not necessarily be helped by money transfers alone. Their problem is deeper and can only be resolved if assistance is provided in a more discretionary manner. Rule-bound public policies are too blunt an instrument and often make matters worse by encouraging self-defeating attitudes. At the same time there are many, such as the frail elderly and the mentally handicapped, who should continue to receive unconditional assistance.

Above all, we need a new focus on understanding the personal life strategies which have proved successful in enabling people to escape from poverty. We need more studies of people who began life in unpromising circumstances, perhaps with a broken family, much neighbourhood crime, drug-taking and alcoholism, but who nevertheless flourished. What is it that enables some who start with disadvantages to overcome their difficulties and how are they different from those who do not? According to *The New Consensus on Family and Welfare,*[2] a report produced by a group of American academics representing all points of the political spectrum, the probability of remaining in poverty is low for those who follow three rules: (1) complete school; (2) once an adult, get married and stay married and (3) stay employed, even at a wage and under conditions below the individual's ultimate aims. In short, the focus of policy for able-bodied people in temporary need of welfare should be on getting them back to work by means of an independence plan which incorporates the lessons learned by those who have successfully risen above their humble origins.

Third, some public policies, directly or indirectly, narrow opportunities to escape from poverty. Particular culprits are high taxes on incomes and savings, and the inadequate integration of taxes and benefits. A comprehensive reform programme is necessary to remove the impediments which make it more difficult for people to advance by their own endeavours. Taxes should be cut to allow workers to keep more of their earnings and the tax system should recognise that the mutual support of the family still remains the best foundation for independence. Taxation of interest on savings has an especially harmful effect on those who want to improve their conditions by saving from earnings. All taxation of income from savings should be abolished.

Fourth, as already argued, there is a need to rebuild the tradition of community without politics which was displaced by the welfare state. To rebuild civil society will require at least two things. Certainly, government should create the space for the re-emergence of a public-but-not-political domain by withdrawing from some activities. But also, without waiting for the government, champions of liberty should establish voluntary associations for assisting the less fortunate and run them in a spirit compatible with liberty.

Recommendations for Public Policy and Private Action

Studies which analyse social problems are expected to recommend solutions, but the common assumption in recent years is that such solutions should be public policy recommendations. It has not always been so. In the not-too-distant past public awareness of a problem would have led, not to a political demand for a government programme, but to a commitment of one's own time and energy to collective but private action. This public-spirited habit has fallen into disrepair and is in urgent need of renewal. Its demise is exemplified by a remark that Tony Blair made in response to a television interviewer's question about what he could do for the deprived. He answered: 'I can't do a damn thing for the deprived unless I'm in government'.[3] In truth, there is a great deal we can do without political power. If anything, the struggle for political power has tended to weaken, even corrupt, the public spirit of old. In the hope of reviving it, some of the recommendations below are for public policies and some for private actions.

1. Restoring the Public-but-not-Political Domain

A good starting point would be the legal framework for voluntary associations. It is of the utmost importance to stimulate the emergence of voluntary associations which are genuinely independent of government, and not only sub-contractors to the state.[4] Governments cannot do much of a positive nature, but they could learn the nineteenth-century lesson that the huge flowering of charity took place against the background of the poor law. The state provided the bare minimum and charitable effort was directed towards helping people to remain free from the poor law. It is, therefore, possible to maintain an official minimum without discouraging private philanthropy. But the government must not be tempted to expand welfare beyond the minimum, because for every step it takes above that minimum it displaces voluntary effort. Such displacement is objectionable, not only because it leads to less adequate care for the poor, but also because, as J.S. Mill argued (see above p. 112) it weakens the character of the people.

We can learn something from our own history about the best method of maintaining a genuine independent sector. During the nineteenth and twentieth centuries the attitude of the state in Britain towards the friendly societies altered radically, thereby helping us to compare the effects of different legal frameworks. There were three main periods: before 1834 the friendly societies were subject to paternalistic supervision by the justices of the peace; between the 1834 Friendly Societies Act and the 1911 National Insurance Act, liberalism was the general rule; and from 1911, paternalism made its return. The heyday of the societies was the period from 1834 to 1911 when the government confined itself to maintaining a framework of law, and requiring disclosure of information to the public, without interfering in the internal management of societies.[5] The lesson is that voluntary associations should be truly independent of the embrace of the state, free to set prices and benefits, to decide whether to function on commercial, mutual or philanthropic lines, and to govern their own affairs under the law of the land.

Charities during the nineteenth century were also subject to light regulation. Indeed they remain so today, but in recent years the chief problem has been that many voluntary associations have come to rely heavily on government grants. Sometimes they have become little more than sub-contractors to the state. As such, they are subject to controls and sometimes fearful of upsetting the authorities lest their grants be withdrawn. A new framework is required which encourages truly independent voluntary associations, which above all means they must rely wholly on private finance. Some of this increased dependence on state finance has inadvertently resulted from efforts to shift services from the public sector to the voluntary, sub-contract sector. This policy has typically been seen as an improvement on the direct employment of officials by the state. But the side-effect has been the infiltration of the voluntary sector by government. Because the public authorities hold the purse strings, they wield too much power.

At present, registered charities enjoy tax concessions. Donations to charities can be made under the Gift Aid scheme, which currently allows them to claim from the Inland Revenue an additional payment equal to one-third of the value of any donation. Gifts can also be made under covenant. Moreover, if charities make a trading profit they are not subject to corporation tax and they also enjoy immunity from VAT on many goods. In addition, charities often receive cash from local or central government either for services rendered under contract, or in the form of general grants.

To develop an independent sector a distinction should be made between organisations whose income comes *only* from private sources, and other organisations whose income could come from a combination of government or private sources. To clarify the distinction, the term 'registered charity' could be reserved for organisations 100 per cent reliant on private finance, and those taking government grants could be called 'registered voluntary associations'.[6] Registered voluntary associations should not enjoy the tax concessions of charities; instead, the tax breaks would be a reward for full reliance on private finance. Legally, registered voluntary associations could trade as non-profit companies or provident associations. The tax-exempt status would need to be withdrawn from organisations which benefit from government grants over a period to allow them to adjust or to work towards full independence as registered charities.

Moreover, to encourage true independence, tax deductions for individual donations should be put on a different basis. At present, under the Gift Aid scheme, an individual making a single donation of £250 or more, results in the charity receiving additional tax relief at the basic rate. Thus, a donation of £300 would allow the charity to claim an additional £100 from the Inland Revenue, making a gross donation of £400. In addition individual donors receive direct tax relief of the difference between the basic rate (25 per cent) and the higher rate (40 per cent). This system should be changed to give individuals direct relief at their marginal rate, so that an individual making a donation of £300 will receive tax relief of either 25 per cent or 40 per cent of his donation. Such tax concessions to individuals in recognition of their generosity would encourage more donations and reduce the risk of state control of the voluntary sector. Similar rules should apply to corporate donations.

The case against tax concessions is that they reduce the tax base. However, the welfare mentality has so seriously weakened civil society, that I believe the use of tax breaks to encourage its renewal to be a higher priority than lowering the general income tax burden. At least tax policy will, for once, be helping to rebuild civil society rather than undermining it.

Having created a new framework for voluntarism, it will be up to the champions of liberty to ensure that a genuinely independent sector develops. Ideally, new voluntary associations will be established conforming to two conditions: refusal to accept government money; and determination to treat beneficiaries, not purely as victims of circumstance, but with the respect due to men and women of character capable of self-improvement and of making a positive contribution in the future. The guiding principle is that practical help is superior to mere almsgiving, whether by charity or the state.

As part of a campaign for the restoration of private welfare, it will be necessary to build up an autonomous voluntary sector without waiting for public policy reform. The more that can be accomplished, the easier it will be to offer a satisfactory answer to the inevitable question: Who will provide welfare if the government withdraws? If the government abruptly withdrew from welfare, there would undoubtedly be some hardship and so there need to be off-the-shelf solutions ready and waiting.

Ideally an organisation should be founded to co-ordinate voluntary associations conforming to this code, and to encourage the new spirit among others. It should try to build a movement of those who take pride in ensuring that vital tasks are undertaken without resort to government.

Business corporations can play a part by reorganising their corporate giving to concentrate resources on voluntary associations which rely 100 per cent on private finance, and by refusing to support voluntary associations which are little more than official offshoots of the government and which in all likelihood see their role as pioneering provision for new 'needs' with the intention of demanding that such needs be met universally out of taxes in due course.

2. *The Benefit System*

One of the main problems we now face is that many people have ingrained habits of dependency. They are not sure whether they will be able to cope without the guiding hand of the state, and some politicians will continue to exploit their feelings, as many already do.

However, there are grounds for optimism now that voices from all points of the political spectrum are warning against the dangers inherent in the present system. Three rival approaches are developing. First, there are defenders of 'the status quo plus a bit of adjustment here and there'. This is the approach of the present government, which wants to retain a combination of national insurance and means-tested benefits. Its approach is indefensible.

Second, there is an emerging socialist critique of which Frank Field is the outstanding representative. It offers a radical and principled criticism of the present system. Field believes that means testing is the root cause of welfare dependency. Because earnings above the income support level are deducted from income support payments, he says, people are encouraged to be dishonest. Therefore, payments should be made as of right and provide an income floor on which people can build. His argument is similar to those who advocate a citizen's income (or basic income guarantee) payable from taxes, but Field insists that the benefit payment should be based on insurance principles, so that it has been 'earned' by payment of earlier contributions. In this manner he hopes to avoid the harmful effects on character of means testing and to eliminate the sense that benefits are 'something for nothing'. Thus, he wants compulsory national insurance to be the norm and means testing to be kept to a minimum. His analysis is explained in more detail below.

The third approach, and the one defended in this publication, calls for the restoration of personal or family responsibility and 'community without politics'. It is not based on a distinction between means testing and guaranteed universal benefits (whether financed from taxes or compulsory insurance). This controversy is a side issue, not least because it is divorced from a wider view of the purpose of public policy, and because debates conducted between enthusiasts for means testing and guaranteed benefits fail to make explicit the assumptions about human nature on which their dispute rests. Once again, Oakeshott's three inseparables provide a useful framework. A society of civil associates is based on three assumptions: first, human nature at its best is about assuming personal responsibility both for self-improvement and making the world a better place for others; second, people are seen to be united, not under leadership, but in acceptance of conditions which allow us all to exercise responsibility; and third government is understood to be the upholder of these conditions, that is, the conditions for liberty. If the purpose of government is to foster liberty, then the task of a welfare system provided by government out of taxes should also be to uphold liberty. It should, therefore, take no actions which diminish personal responsibility, and implement only those measures which are intended to restore personal independence.

From this standpoint, compulsory insurance is not sufficiently respectful of individual responsibility in two particular ways: first, by requiring people to provide against contingencies through insurance it suppresses other methods, such as saving or capital investment, when it is from such diversity of provision that we learn better ways of meetings needs; and second, it fosters immaturity by encouraging reliance on the political authorities.

People should be free to provide against contingencies as they believe best, and insurance is only one of the methods they may choose. This is more than a theoretical point. Historically, the imposition of compulsory insurance in 1911 destroyed some of the finest organisations which have ever developed, the friendly societies.[7] The government of the day based the National Insurance Act on a mechanical view of need, enforcing contributions and paying benefits, but disregarding the essential spirit of the friendly societies.

As well as providing benefits, the friendly societies were also voluntary associations for the enrichment of life and for the promotion of the best in people. But under the 1911 Act the government stripped out the obvious technical services and treated the vital life-improving functions as subsidiary to the benefits. It disregarded all non-pecuniary friendly society services because the ruling politicians were under the influence of a low view of human character and potential. National insurance was calculated to 'buy' working class votes and to prove the government's concern for 'social reform'. The benefits were financed from bogus insurance in the hope of not alienating middle-class taxpayers who were reluctant to pay more.[8] Lloyd George told voters the infantile story that they would receive 'ninepence for fourpence' because male contributions were fourpence, employers threepence and the government twopence. The benefits also became separate elements for which a person qualified or not, whereas the friendly societies at their best saw themselves as associations of persons providing what a modern marketing expert might call a 'comprehensive independence package'. This combination of services had value over and above any individual element.

The second weakness of compulsory insurance is that it does not take into account the impact of compulsion on character development. By taking over in 1911 the vital function of preserving personal independence through the payment of insurance contributions to voluntary associations, the state diminished opportunities for strengthening character. And this remains the defect in Frank Field's scheme. It appears that he has failed to see this drawback because he concentrates too narrowly on the disadvantages of means testing. However, the moral improvements which he sincerely wants will only result from directly fostering institutions which promote the honesty, thrift, hard-work and dedication to the common good he hopes for. By displacing voluntary co-operative effort, the state achieves the exact opposite.

Here I must digress for a moment to avoid misunderstanding. One of the dominant assumptions of nineteenth- and twentieth-century liberals is that actions by the state subtract from individual freedom. In its extreme form, every state action is assumed to displace or prohibit a potential individual action. This attitude became entrenched largely as a result of Bentham's influence. The counter view, and the typical view of liberals before Bentham, was that law does not always replace freedom but rather creates it. As Adam Ferguson, a contemporary of Adam Smith put it:

> The establishment of a just and effectual government is of all circumstances in civil society the most essential to freedom: that everyone is justly said to be free in proportion as the government under which he resides is sufficiently powerful to protect him, at the same time that it is sufficiently restrained and limited to prevent the abuse of this power.[9]

Hayek tried to revive this earlier view. When the law tells us what the state will uphold, it allows us to exercise our personal responsibility for bringing about 'the best' as we see it. That is, the actions of the state *may* subtract from individual freedom but they do not always do so. And the public policy issue is to distinguish between those state actions that uphold liberty and those which undermine it. Hayek suggests the following question as a guide: Which public policy measures uphold the opportunity for unknown persons to do good in their own way and which make people mere instruments of government? That is, he asks whether the state is using people as instruments for the ends of the rulers or whether it is creating the conditions for people to pursue their own diverse ends. Liberty in this view does not only mean doing whatever any given person might want, but assuming personal responsibility for being a better individual and improving the world around us. Thus, the view I am recommending should not be confused with blanket animosity to government as such, but it is essential that the state does not weaken human potential for the exercise of responsibility.

The underlying belief is that we should take personal or family responsibility for self-support throughout our lives, including provision against foreseeable contingencies like ill-health and certainties like getting older and death. If the government assumes responsibility for such provision it treats people as perpetual children incapable of providing for themselves. It also reduces the quality of human life to the extent that fulfilment rests on facing up to and overcoming life's difficulties. Moreover, by diminishing opportunities to strengthen character and enhance skills through facing challenges, people are rendered less able to discharge their duties as citizens, further reinforcing the claims of paternalists that the 'common people' require supervision. Individuals whose qualities have not been tested and stretched are less able to see through the false promises of manipulative politicians and to stand in independent judgement of government, as democracy requires.

Three types of benefit should be reformed in the first instance. First, those that provide against insurable contingencies, like ill health or certainties like death, should be restored to civil society.

Second, the systems for supporting people out of work but capable of working should be put on a more personal footing. At present they are primarily income maintenance systems; instead they should become personalised services for the restoration of independence.

Third, provision for income in old age should become a personal responsibility with the state retaining a role only in providing a safety net.

Because of its complexity, pension provision will be the subject of a separate study. Here I will concentrate on the benefits that are privately insurable and on assistance for people out of work.

Insurable Contingencies

We know from past experience that private arrangements for insurance against loss of income during illness worked well, and the aim of public policy should be to restore these services to civil society. The immediate candidates are statutory sick pay, short-term incapacity benefit, and long-term incapacity benefit.

In the past sick pay was provided by friendly societies far more satisfactorily than by governments. Even Lloyd George, who had fallen under the sway of Bismarckian corporatism, introduced the 1911 National Insurance Act in the House of Commons by expressing admiration for the friendly societies. He claimed that the legislation was intended to extend to everyone what the vast majority of people had already done for themselves. A variety of different schemes were on offer to suit different needs, some combining saving and insurance and others based on simple insurance.[10] According to Beveridge, three aspirations contributed to the formation of friendly societies: the first was the desire for security in sickness, the second a wish to avoid a pauper funeral, and the third to save for emergencies, old age or a major purchase.[11] The national societies with branches concentrated on sick pay, medical care and funeral benefit, whereas the local dividing societies put greater stress on saving and shared any annual surplus among members.[12] The weakness of the dividing principle was that, as the members grew older, the benefits got larger and the annual surplus smaller. But, for some, this lack of actuarial calculation was also its advantage. By paying a higher contribution than was strictly necessary, members knew that the benefits would usually be covered and that any surplus would be returned to them.[13]

The same desire for a balance between saving and security in sickness and old age led to the formation of deposit and

Holloway societies. The National Deposit Friendly Society was the largest of its type. Each member made a contribution which went partly to a common fund for sick pay and partly to a personal interest-bearing account. Members could choose the size of their contribution so long as it was no less than 2s per month and no more than 20s. This contribution then determined the benefit: the daily rate of sick benefit was the same as the monthly rate of contribution. Sick pay was drawn partly from the common fund and partly from the member's personal account and was payable until the member's personal account was exhausted. For example, sick pay for males who joined between the ages of 16 and 30 was paid 25 per cent from their personal account and 75 per cent from the common fund. This meant that a person who did not experience much illness would accumulate a large surplus by retirement age. Members who were ill for long periods could exhaust their personal account, but they received 'grace pay' (75 per cent of benefit for those who joined before age 30) for the same period that sick pay had already been drawn.[14]

Holloway societies also combined saving and sick pay but in a different way. The contribution was substantially more than was necessary for sick pay and the whole payment went into a common fund. Each year the surplus was divided equally and credited to personal accounts which earned interest. Holloway societies also allowed an individual to increase his share of the distributed surplus by holding more than one share in the society (up to ten shares). The essential idea was to pay more than was necessary for sick pay in order to build up a surplus for old age. However, unlike the National Deposit Friendly Society, it was not possible to run out of sick pay. The best known Holloway society (which still functions successfully today) is the Tunbridge Wells Equitable.

Quite apart from their success in providing schemes to suit all types, the societies also proved effective at controlling fraud. Local control was the key to success. The Prudential Assurance Company, the largest of the industrial assurance companies, had to abandon sick pay because, according to the evidence of its secretary to the Royal Commission on Friendly Societies in 1873, 'after five years' experience we found we were unable to cope with the fraud that was practised'. The centralised friendly societies also found it more difficult to control fraud. The Hearts of Oak Benefit Society, the largest and most efficient of the centralised societies, had no branches and dispensed all benefits from its head office. Its rate of sickness was significantly higher than that of the societies with local branches such as the Foresters and the Oddfellows. During the eight years 1884-91, for instance, the sickness experience of the Hearts of Oak was over 30 per cent above that of the Manchester Unity of Oddfellows.[15]

This problem arises when beneficiaries no longer feel a real sense of involvement. Where local branches administered sick pay the members knew who was paying—it was the members themselves. But if 'head office' made the payment, it was possible to entertain the illusion that someone else was bearing the cost. And many centralised insurers had no better answer to this illusion than today's government departments. Some centralised friendly societies, such as the National Deposit Friendly Society, combined saving with insurance to overcome the difficulty, but it was the local societies and branches of the affiliated orders whose members felt they had a real stake in the organisation to an extent which proved sufficient, not only to discourage selfishness, but also to build a genuine sense of fraternity. There was some fraud, but for many members a spirit of brotherhood did guide their conduct. Some would not claim sick pay at all, however strong their entitlement, and of those who did, the great majority only claimed their due. Thus, the affiliated friendly societies handled the problem of fraud far more effectively than does modern officialdom.

How is sick pay provided today? Since April 1995 people incapable of work due to illness have been able to claim statutory sick pay for 28 weeks, after which they must apply for incapacity benefit. In 1992/93 sickness benefit (now replaced), statutory sick pay and invalidity benefit (now incapacity benefit) cost £7,125 million.[16] The government has tightened up the administration of incapacity benefit in the hope of reducing fraud, but it has chosen to rely on more stringent medical examinations rather than on fostering moral responsibility. A more radical remedy is needed.

Transitional Measures

How could the ultimate objective of replacing compulsory national insurance by voluntary provision be accomplished? Existing commitments would need to be honoured, but from a given date no new benefit payments could be made. Expenditure on existing benefits could come from general tax revenues and would diminish over time. In addition, the Government should guarantee that all reductions in benefit expenditure will be returned in the form of cuts in national insurance contributions, and if spending reductions exceed revenue from national insurance, that taxes will be cut. This would restore income to people thus enabling them to take out private insurance.

Private insurance for sick pay should not be compulsory, not least because insurance is not the only method of protection against contingencies. Many people may prefer simple saving, or investment in shares, or to purchase property or durable goods which can be sold if the need arises.

The main public policy problem is how to cater for people who might want insurance but are not insurable. A few people with pre-existing conditions would not pass insurers' medical examinations. There are several possible ways of ensuring that people in this group do not lose out. In the first place, it should be acknowledged that insurance is not necessarily the best remedy for every individual. However, there are possible methods of including everyone within insurers' schemes.

The government could forbid insurers from taking pre-existing conditions into account and to overcome the initial impact on insurers' reserves it could make a single once-for-all transfer payment from tax revenues. Alternatively, those in work with pre-existing conditions could be grouped in a 'risk pool' and allowed to choose their own private insurer. There are a number of successful examples of risk pools for medical expenses insurance in America, and the model could be adapted for income replacement during illness. Insurers might, for example, charge a market premium and receive an agreed subsidy from public funds, or the government might run a public scheme for uninsurable people in disregard of insurance principles. A third possibility would be a legal requirement for insurers to accept a quota of people with pre-existing conditions, based on their market share. If an organisation fell below its quota it would pay a levy to the government at a price set to discourage free-riding. Under such arrangements everyone would be able to purchase insurance, but would not be compelled to do so.

A fourth possibility would be to adapt the old model of the provident dispensary. Low premiums were charged to allow the poor to pay what they could afford towards the cost of medical care, and better off people paid into the provident fund to subsidise poorer members. That is, the provident dispensaries were funded partly by the contributions of beneficiaries and partly by the charitable donations of the (non-benefiting) honorary members.[17] Historically, these organisations developed to provide medical care, but the principle could be adapted to cater for people unable to obtain insurance. Private individuals could pay an additional premium over and above what the beneficiary could afford. Would the idea catch on? The British people have traditionally been generous and many may well be attracted to support provident associations. Today, organisations which have an ethical as well as a commercial purpose are already popular, including unit trusts promising 'ethical investments'.

Thus, provision for income replacement during illness would be returned to civil society. There is already a flourishing private sector offering sick pay, or permanent health insurance, as it is now called. These commercial insurers and the friendly societies would be in a strong position to fill in gaps left by the retreating state.

The government's role would be transformed from one of responsibility for everyone, to ensuring that no one is left out. It becomes a 'guarantor' rather than a 'compulsory provider'. The mistake in 1911 was to enforce a single uniform scheme for all persons. It was right that the government should concern itself with people left out of voluntary insurance schemes, but it should have tried to help them without taking over the whole system and without assuming that the government should only assist by means of insurance.

Out of Work But Fit For Work

According to C.S. Loch, Mill's sentiments described above (p. 122) helped to inspire the formation of the Charity Organisation Society (COS) in the 1860s.[18] For Loch, the work of charity ought to be more than 'disorganised sentiment'. It should be a counterpart to the state safety net. Mere almsgiving was insufficient, and the charity of the COS required knowledge and the commitment of time to the person being helped. The focus of the COS on the individual has in more recent times been presented as a callous philosophy, but it emphasised the distinction between the undemanding kindness of giving money, and the thoughtful and more committed kindness of taking the trouble to discover the full personal circumstances and to ensure that the help given was likely to restore independence. Those today who accuse the COS of lacking concern typically demand only that *other* people give cash support. They fail to see the superiority of personalised, direct practical help.

We need to go back to the beginning of this century to discover the last occasion on which this philosophy was clearly understood. Mill's doctrine influenced the Majority Report of the Royal Commission on the Poor Laws of 1909 which sought to combine state financial support with practical help and guidance by voluntary organisations, in the hope of maintaining a humane minimum without increasing dependency.

The Majority Report recommended the abolition of the general workhouse and for separate provision of residential relief to be made for different types of need, including children, the aged or infirm, the sick and the able-bodied. It also proposed that the Boards of Guardians be replaced in each county or county borough by a Public Assistance Authority (PAA) which would exercise overall supervision of relief. The actual work of dealing with applications and administering help would be dealt with by Public Assistance Committees (PACs) which initially would coincide with the former poor law unions.

In the area of each Public Assistance Authority a Voluntary Aid Council was to be established, consisting of representatives of charities, the PAA, friendly societies, trade unions, the clergy and others. In turn, it would form Voluntary Aid Committees (VACs), which would aid people in distress referred to them by the PACs. It was intended that the VACs would attempt first to strengthen family ties and local bonds by encouraging family and friends to give support. At the heart of the work of the Voluntary Aid Committees was to be the voluntary worker or friendly visitor, who would visit, assess and offer practical help as well as moral and prudential guidance. This scheme was designed for different circumstances, but its principles remain applicable today, above all the policy of restricting government assistance to a low cash payment and, in all cases where there is any chance of effective personal assistance, referring individuals to a voluntary association.

The current position in Britain is this. From April 1996 unemployment benefit will be replaced by the Jobseeker's Allowance. Income support for people out of work is also to be abolished in April 1996 and replaced by the Jobseeker's Allowance.

Under the new scheme, claimants will have to enter into a Jobseeker's Agreement which will commit them to taking agreed steps to find work. For those who have paid sufficient national insurance contributions, Jobseeker's Allowance will be paid without a means test for six months (unemployment benefit was paid for 12 months, after 3 days out of work). After that, means tests will apply. One criticism of the pre-April-1996 system is that people are discouraged from taking part-time work as a pathway back to full-time work. Consequently, recipients of Jobseeker's Allowance who work part-time will be able to save up to £1,000 of their pay, which they can take as a 'back to work bonus' when they resume full-time employment.

Even this modest measure has been described as harsh, but in many European countries, particularly those with a social-democratic tradition, people out of work come under strong pressure to assume a place in the workforce. Sweden's system, for example, is based on the 'employment' rather than the 'cash assistance' principle, and the government employment service ensures that everyone is assisted back into work.[19] The tradition in countries such as Germany and Denmark is similar. Far from being seen as harsh, the expectation of work is taken for granted.

The British Jobseeker's Allowance is a step in the right direction, but because it is to be implemented by public officials it inevitably will take on a mechanical character. Frank Field has made a similar point. The Benefits Agency, he says, should become primarily concerned with constructing exits and the Jobseeker's Allowance should not be a mechanical test, but a personalised programme of building skills.[20] He concedes that existing staff are unsuitable for the task, but believes that the Benefits Agency can transform itself sufficiently to implement the new approach.[21] The Swiss have managed to devise a local welfare system based on local cantons,[22] but in the absence of a cantonal tradition it seems to me unlikely that the reform will succeed in Britain unless voluntary agencies are involved.

Quite apart from this problem, the extension of national insurance recommended by Field is not feasible because unemployment is not strictly insurable due to the difficulty of distinguishing between voluntary and involuntary unemployment. For this reason, unemployment benefit was not provided commercially, but only by a few trade unions for their own members. Most people adopted a variety of alternative methods of provision, not least saving. The friendly societies and many trade unions preferred to provide 'travelling benefit', that is they assisted with the extra cost of searching for work, but did not provided unconditional cash assistance. Norman Tebbit famously pointed out that his father's generation would have 'got on their bike' to find work. No less important, they would typically have joined a friendly society or trade union which would provide mutual support if the day of hardship came. They cycled to distant towns, not to tramp the cold streets alone, but to meet the welcoming (secret) handshake of the local lodge secretary.

I have already argued that in a free society compulsion should be kept to a minimum. However, it is true that a free economy encourages change in the interests of all, and in the short run there are undoubtedly casualties as industries come and go. A compromise approach might be to require a compulsory contribution sufficient to pay the Jobseeker's Allowance for 6 months. The self-employed would not need to pay and could not claim. Moreover, individuals should be free to contract out, so long as they sign a statement accepting full personal responsibility for self-support during the six months for which Jobseeker's Allowance is payable. They would also not be eligible for income support during that time. Something along these lines would be a defensible compromise, but the ideal would be to wind up national insurance and transform income support to facilitate private provision, the challenge to which I now turn.

Reforming the Income Support System

How should income support be reformed? The main conditions for income support are:

1. The applicant's income must be less than the 'applicable amount' (that is, the needs recognised by the benefits agency) (see below).
2. Savings and other capital should be worth £8,000 or less. (Some capital, including the claimant's home and personal possessions, are ignored.)

3. Neither the claimant nor his or her partner must be in full-time paid work, defined as 16 hours work per week (until 1992 it was 24 hours).
4. The claimant should not be in full-time education, although studying part-time may be possible.
5. The claimant should be 16 or older (children aged 16-17 have to satisfy extra rules).
6. Claimants should be signing on as available for work and actively seeking employment (unless they are not required to do so).
7. The claimant must satisfy the 'habitual residence test' and be present in Great Britain.[23]

The 'applicable amount' is calculated by adding the personal allowance and any premiums (plus permitted housing costs for some home owners and housing benefit for rent payers). The personal allowances and premiums are set out below.

Income Support Applicable Amounts, 1995-96

Personal Allowances	
under 18 (usual rate)	£28.00
under 18 (in some circumstances)	£36.80
aged 18-24	£36.80
aged 25 and over	£46.50
Single Parent	
under 18 (usual rate)	£28.00
under 18 (in some circumstances)	£36.80
aged 18 and over	£46.50
Couple	
both under 18	£55.55
one/both over 18	£73.00
Dependent children	
under 11	£15.95
aged 11-15	£23.40
aged 16-17	£28.00
aged 18	£36.80

Income Support Applicable Amounts, 1995-96

Premiums	
Family	£10.25
Lone Parent	£ 5.20
Pensioner	
single	£18.60
couple	£28.05
Enhanced Pensioner	
single	£20.70
couple	£30.95
Higher Pensioner	
single	£25.15
couple	£35.95
Disability	
single	£19.80
couple	£28.30
Severe Disability	
single	£35.05
couple (if one qualifies)	£35.05
couple (if both qualify)	£70.10
Disabled child	£19.80

The Alternative

The first principle is that income support should only be claimed as an absolute last resort. It should be a matter of honour to avoid claiming and to rely on savings wherever they exist. Consequently, it should be necessary to spend all capital, and all income of any kind whatsoever should be deducted from the applicable amount (unless opting for support from a voluntary association as described below). Means testing should be applied only to the immediate family (man, wife and children), and not to other relatives.

To ensure a focus on the development of personalised help, claimants should have the option of receiving assistance from a voluntary organisation instead of the Benefits Agency. The voluntary organisation would be free to support individuals as it believed best, using its own money. But, individuals would not be legally required to spend their savings or have their earnings deducted from benefit if they opted for support from a voluntary association instead of the Benefits Agency.

Such associations would concentrate on devising personalised schemes to help people back on their feet, and would need to be free to devise policies on savings and earnings most consistent with the early return to independence of each person under its temporary care. They would be able to arrange pathways back to independence through part-time work or training or personal morale-building without the benefit system producing perverse incentives. At present, for example, a person on income support has no real reason to take part-time work because he would lose the bulk of his benefit. A face-to-face relationship with a voluntary association worker will not have the same corrupting effect. All assistance will be discretionary and subject to mutual agreement. In such a personal relationship, mutual respect, honour and good faith have a chance, but an arms-length relationship with a public official bound by rules and regulations encourages dishonesty, bad faith and 'working the system'.

As a public body, the Benefits Agency must act according to rules, and the ability of officials to exercise discretion is rightly limited. But discretion is exactly what is needed. Consider just one example, the enforcement of the 'voluntary employment deduction' rule.

In certain circumstances, an individual can be classified as 'voluntarily unemployed', disqualified from receiving unemployment benefit and paid a reduced rate of income support for up to 26 weeks. In such a case, income support is reduced by 40 per cent of the personal allowance for a single claimant. Thus, if the rate was £28.00, the deduction would be £11.20. According to the Child Poverty Action Group guide, individuals are treated as voluntarily unemployed if they have:

- lost their job because of misconduct; or
- left their job voluntarily without good cause; or
- without good cause refused to apply for, or take, a suitable job; or
- without good cause failed to take up a reasonable opportunity of employment; or

- without good cause failed to follow reasonable recommendations made to help them find suitable employment; or
- lost a place on an approved training scheme such as Youth Training, because of misconduct, or given up a place without good cause; or
- without good cause, refused or failed to take up training approved by the Employment Service (such as 18-year-olds who refuse to take up a YT place).

The CPAG explains the complexities involved in interpreting 'good cause'. A job could reasonably be refused if:

- the work might cause serious harm to health, or excessive physical or mental stress; or
- there was a religious or conscientious objection; or
- the claimant was responsible for looking after someone else; or
- the time it would take to get to work and back is excessive (the CPAG suggests more than one hour each way as an indication of an excessive journey); or
- the costs that would necessarily arise are too high (child care costs are not taken into account, and low pay does not itself make a job unsuitable, but the CPAG advises people to argue that they have 'good cause' for refusal if the pay is less than income support after travel); or
- it is work of a kind they do not usually do and if the individual is within their 'permitted period' of 13 weeks after first claiming benefit; or
- the job is available only because of a trade dispute; or
- it is not related to the type of work for which the claimant has just finished training for at least two-months (this argument can only be used for four weeks after the course ends); or
- the job is one the claimant found out about himself, unless he was also formally told about the job at the unemployment benefit office, or worked for the same employer less than a year ago and the pay and conditions are only as good as before.[24]

These passages in the CPAG guide show how difficult it is to make such decisions at arms length. The reality is that matters of such complexity can only be resolved face-to-face in relationships based on mutual respect. The advice produced by the CPAG and similar organisations takes the form of recommended lines of argument that experience has shown to be effective in maximising the individual's 'take' from the taxpayer. Appealing against unfavourable decisions is encouraged and the general tone of the advice seems unconsciously to assume that the highest moral principle is: claim all you can get away with. Under such a regime and given such encouragement there is endless scope for acting in bad faith. For this reason, such judgements should be made within personal relationships based on a shared commitment by helper and recipient to an early return to independence.

Naturally, there would need to be safeguards against overzealous voluntary organisations. It should always remain open to an individual to revert back to Benefits Agency support, following a period of notice, or to switch to another voluntary agency, again after a period of notice. It is likely that such safeguards will encourage some people to choose the apparently softest option, but the paramount consideration is to ensure that anyone with the potential for independence can find the right sort of help and to keep compulsion to a minimum.

Benefits and Family Breakdown

What should be done about the special problem of family breakdown? One approach is that of Charles Murray. He accepts that there is no single right answer and urges that different American states be permitted to experiment. He hopes that some will adopt a plan for compulsory work urged by social commentator, Mickey Kaus, whose scheme is based on experience gained during the Depression.[25] Murray's own view is that benefits should be cut. He recommends that those already on benefits should be allowed to retain them and that any new policy should be confined to the never-married, and not applied to the divorced or widowed. Initially, he also argues that his reforms should be limited to teenage never-married mothers, and only extended later to all never-married mothers.

They should be given one year's notice that all benefits contingent on having a baby are to be cancelled, especially Aid to Families with Dependent Children (AFDC). However, never-married mothers would retain food stamps, public housing and Medicaid. Ideally, Murray wants a negative income tax scheme which makes one payment that does not vary according to the number of children. In addition, he wants never-married mothers to be encouraged to have their babies adopted, but without coercion. Never-married pregnant women and never-married mothers should also be offered the chance, but not required, to live in group homes where there would be a degree of supervision, personal support and mutual assistance. Finally, he wants child-neglect laws to be enforced to ensure that those who refuse to live in supervised homes do not harm their children.

Many who share Murray's belief that the ideal is for all children to be raised by two good parents wherever possible, do not, however, favour cutting benefits. They oppose benefit cutting because it would cause too much hardship and leave too much to chance. Instead, they recommend attaching conditions to benefit, particularly a work requirement.

How should Britain proceed? The first target should be the fathers of illegitimate children, rather than the mothers, who after all, do have custody of the children. Fathers should be subject to the most severe measures. If they are not willing to marry the mother, or if she is not willing to marry them, they should be required to pay the full cost of maintenance. Decisions about parentage and the setting of payments should be made in a court of law and enforced by the Child Support Agency, which should confine its work to pursuing fathers of illegitimate children and become accountable to the courts rather than to a government minister.

Divorced men should be supervised by the courts as previously. In divorce cases fault should be taken into account in awarding custody of the children and making maintenance awards. These are complex and delicate matters of law and fact which are the proper province of the courts of justice. An administrative agency can justly enforce a court decision but at present the CSA has quasi-judicial powers which it has shown itself wholly unfit to exercise.

Fathers of illegitimate children who are low paid should be legally required to hand over all their earnings above the income support applicable amount and have all their savings and any non-essential possessions confiscated up to the amount required. If they give up work to avoid payment they should be compelled to work at special centres as a condition of receiving benefit. It may be necessary in a few cases to make this work obligation especially burdensome, perhaps by requiring performance of hard labour for up to ten hours a day. If necessary, we should not shrink from such measures. To father a child and to refuse to take responsibility should be clearly marked out as one of the lowest things a man can do.

At present a never-married mother is required to disclose the father's identity and failure to do so can lead to her benefit being reduced, unless she faces a threat of violence. This provision encourages violence, or the pretence of it, and should be abolished. Three new criminal offences should be introduced: failure by a father to register the birth of his child should be a serious criminal offence; threatening the mother with violence to conceal the father's identity should also be a serious offence, punishable by a substantial jail sentence; and failure to pay maintenance as ordered should become a criminal offence, which could lead to an indefinite jail sentence, unless the father undertakes to resume payment. These measures will strike many as severe, and that is the intention. They are likely to bring about a substantial behavioural change by men.

At the turn of the century it used to be argued that the burden should be put on the woman to avoid pregnancy, because she would be least able to escape the consequences. The reasoning was that, knowing that the man could more easily get off scot-free, the female would be less likely to take risks. This rationale no longer makes sense now that condoms are widely and cheaply available. The condom reduces the risk of disease and pregnancy and it is a male responsibility to use one and use it properly. The clear message the law should send is that any man contemplating sex outside marriage must be prepared to face the consequences of his actions. It is up to him to take contraceptive precautions. He will not be able to argue: 'Well she told me she was on the pill. How was I to know?' The man should be held responsible in all circumstances, without exception.

We need also to reform the welfare system. Benefits for never-married mothers should not be cut, but the work test applied to unemployed claimants should also be applied to never-married mothers, once their first child reaches the age of two. It should not apply to formerly married women.

It is likely that such a system will be more costly for the taxpayer in the short run, because it will be necessary to subsidise child care in some cases. This, however, is a price worth paying, because the result of taking no action will be increased family breakdown and increased reliance on benefits. The lone-parent family is neither an economically, nor an emotionally, viable lifestyle. It takes two parents to raise children, at least one of whom must work. Moreover, once established, the cost of the scheme would fall as fewer people chose to rely on benefits in response to the very different signals being sent by the benefit system.

At present young girls contemplating the possibility of being made pregnant are aware that the result will be a free house and an income to match earnings from employment, without the trouble of working. A girl who has just sat her 'A' levels and who hopes to continue her studies would not find the lifestyle appealing, but for girls of limited ability and ambition such a lifestyle may appear more attractive than the alternative. If, however, the future promises a five-day working week plus caring for the child alone in the evenings and weekends, fewer will choose it.

The work requirement as a condition of benefit has another strength compared with Murray's scheme. He leaves existing never-married mothers unscathed. Yet many are bringing up their children negligently, a cost that will be borne by those children throughout their lives, and which is likely to rebound on the community in the form of increased crime. Under these proposals they will be expected to work.

Again, much depends on the emergence of voluntary agencies (registered voluntary associations and genuinely independent charities) to develop innovative methods of restoring independence and providing help. Their essential task is to find ways of treating people as individuals, with care, attention and judgement.

While pregnant and before their first child is two, never-married mothers should be encouraged to live either with their parents, or in supervised accommodation, preferably provided by voluntary associations that will take responsibility for bringing out the best in mother and baby. Many such institutions existed historically and continue to do so today. They offer a supervised lifestyle but the beneficiaries will be guided by people totally dedicated to their well-being. An example of a successful modern scheme is that of Sister Connie Driscoll in Chicago. She has run the St Martin de Porres House of Hope centre for homeless mothers and their children for 12 years in one of Chicago's most violent districts. Some 85 per cent of the mothers are drug addicts on arrival, but she claims that after an average stay of about seven months, 95 per cent leave her care with a job, their own home and free from drugs. Since opening, over 9,000 mothers have lived in the hostel.[26]

Adoption should also be encouraged, but not required.

Moralism and Social Security

There are still many who harbour doubts about the application of moral principles to public policy. Typically they will say, 'Yes, of course, a person should lead a moral life, and I do myself, but I do not wish to impose my values on other people'. It is often difficult to progress beyond this reluctance to 'impose values on other people', as if any social pressure was always illegitimate.

First, this assertion confuses self-restraint and external control, as argued in Chapter 3. If we accept that we should restrain ourselves in the interests of others, how do we decide what other people's interests are? Do the values that guide our self-restraint come purely from within, or are they in some sense a shared responsibility? I argued in Chapter 3 that they are 'common property' and that if we want a free society we must accept the burden of working together—but without resort to the political system—to uphold a set of shared values, including liberty itself. In any event, we send moral signals to others whether we are conscious of it or not. The person who insists he does not want to 'impose values' unavoidably sends signals of approval or disapproval, as we all do. And at the very least, as parents we should surely take care that our moral signals to our children are the right ones, consistent with freedom.

The further question is, what are the proper limits of social pressure? Plainly, there are some limits. A society suffocated by constant frowns, glares, sideways glances and raised eyebrows would not be attractive. But none of those who insist that family breakdown is a proper concern for the public hope to 'impose' a wide array of their values on other people. Usually they hope to assert only one, namely the obligation to raise your own children in a manner consistent with their well-being.

More important still, the dispute about family values does not involve a clear-cut choice between imposition or non-imposition, for the man who creates new human life and then refuses to be a good father—even to the extent of not being present under the same roof as his child, let alone offering financial and emotional support—is already imposing *his* values on the child, not to mention the other people he expects to fill the gap he has left. The list includes the mother, other relatives, taxpayers, teachers, social workers and more, who will be called upon to help.

Thus, there is already 'imposition' and the purpose—and the effect—of legal imposition of duties on the man is to reduce the sum total of imposition in society. The intention of my proposals is to create circumstances in which children are more likely to be brought up by devoted parents.

To concede that the state may impose this duty is not to set off down a slippery slope. There are, indeed, slippery slopes and sometimes we have to defend liberty on less than ideal battlegrounds to avoid setting a dangerous precedent. But to insist on a father's duty to his own child does not establish a precedent that can be used to justify any number of other intrusions by governments. Liberals should not, therefore, feel impelled to defend the 'right to irresponsibility' in the false belief that they are guarding against the enforcement of laws incompatible with liberty. The creation of new human life is special; and the obligations of parents are special.

But not everyone who is reluctant to contemplate the imposition of obligations on parents is deterred by abstract concern with setting a precedent. Sometimes the stumbling-block is anxiety about particular modern moral controversies, two of which stand out from the crowd: abortion and homosexuality.

If the law imposes obligations on fathers will homosexuality and abortion be next in the frame? The general principle in a free society is that we should accept that the law will not always enforce our own moral ideals. We must settle in such cases for the freedom to express our open approval or disapproval, without aspiring to resort to law. Take abortion. It is legal on medical grounds up to a stipulated number of weeks after conception. Many oppose it in all circumstances. They should be free to put their view, and enthusiasts for abortion on demand should tolerate them; and vice versa. There is no consensus for further legal reform at present. Similarly, no case for persecuting homosexuals can be built on the enforcement of parental obligations either legally or by means of social pressure.

Creating new human life is in class of its own. To opt to take no responsibility for a helpless infant, when we have learnt from the hard experience of ages past that the damage to the child will be serious and lasting, is not a right. It is simply selfish and the state can justly impose a duty of support on the parents in such cases. As Adam Smith understood, the decision to have a child is a decision to make a contribution to the continuance of the civilisation to which we belong. It entails a commitment to the future and requires that we assume responsibility for passing on to the next generation the virtues indispensable to freedom. The man who impregnates a woman, only to desert both mother and child, is putting two fingers in the air, not only to them, but also to the very civilisation which has nurtured him from infancy.

A Comparison with Frank Field's Proposals

Field's analysis of the welfare problem has a certain amount in common with mine. He accepts that character is the key and is aware of the historical debate that took place in Britain around the turn of the century, when 'social collectivism', or what I have been calling 'community without politics' was understood to be different from 'political collectivism'.[27] He reaffirms the COS view and wishes in certain respects to restore it.[28]

Field is especially courageous in his remarks about never-married mothers and accepts that national insurance should not be extended to single parents.[29] Political correctness, he says, has prevented the harm done by lone parents from being exposed.[30] Single mothers should be expected to work, and not 'left alone' till their children are 16 as at present. Child-care and training should be provided for single mothers and the skills of their children should also be improved.[31]

However, his main analysis identifies the welfare problem as the result of a Tory move from national insurance to means testing.[32] He particularly dislikes means testing because it penalises people with savings while giving money to claimants who have not saved. It also penalises people who find work, he says, by taking away their benefit.

In one sense his point is valid, but a means tested system in reality only penalises work because the benefit payment is high compared with earnings. The underlying problem is the expectation that the money ought to be provided with or without work. In the past it was considered to be 'letting the side down' to take from others without putting something back, and those who complain that they are being punished for working because benefit is reduced to take account of earnings, ought instead to take pride in their self-reliance. Similarly, those who complain that they have to spend their savings down to the £8,000 limit to qualify, and who argue that his requirement discourages thrift, have adopted the mentality of 'rights without duties'. Instead, they should feel pride in their independence. Field's response is to agree with them and to find a way of paying them without expecting reliance on savings or without deducting earnings from benefits. But this approach concedes too much to the ethos of dependency. It is wrong to encourage the illusion of rights without duties.

Field pursues his analysis by showing that, since 1951, fewer unemployed people have been eligible for unemployment benefit. In 1951 67 per cent were eligible, whereas by 1994 it was only 17 per cent.[33] Adequacy of benefits is not the problem, he says, but non-payment of contributions, and his remedy is to reform contribution requirements to allow more people to be entitled to unconditional benefits.[34]

To his credit, he warns against the traditional 'centre-left' strategy of raising national insurance benefits because, he argues, it would be too expensive to do so.[35] And no less important, he disassociates himself from compulsory redistribution of income. National insurance should not be an excuse for concealed equalisation.[36]

His programme has four main points which he expects it will take 20 years to implement:

1. Phase out means tests.
2. Phase in more national insurance.
3. Transform income support into a more 'pro-active' system.
4. Provide pensions by means of a public-private partnership.[37]

Field recommends the establishment of two corporations: one for national insurance and one for pensions. Membership of the governing bodies should reflect the payment of contributions. On this formula, membership of the national insurance corporation today would be 49 per cent employers, 31 per cent employees, 3 per cent the self-employed and 17 per cent government.[38] The government would initially determine contributions but thereafter it would only have a veto. It would pay the contributions of the long-term sick, the unemployed and carers.[39]

His reform strategy is not only distorted by a reluctance to criticise some bad attitudes, but also by political considerations, particularly because he goes out of his way to harness the self-interest of the middle class.[40] The chief reality for them, he believes, is their sense of job insecurity and, for this reason, a national insurance scheme should have considerable appeal.[41] Field cites the Webb's success in harnessing jingoism to their campaign for a 'national minimum' and argues that today middle-class job insecurity is the most deeply felt public sentiment available for exploitation.[42] Unfortunately, this is the same manipulative political thinking that led to the original argument for national insurance. It is flawed for the same reason. It does not seek to strengthen character. The more important question is how to appeal to the best in people.

Field calls means testing the 'poor law tradition', but the current system is not that of the poor law, which is typically caricatured as about 'less-eligibility'. The poor law had existed since medieval times and its existence is a tribute to the humanity of the British people who would not allow anyone to fall below a certain point, regardless of their moral conduct. The nineteenth century debate about whether it should be more strict or more lax is not radically different from the modern debate. The issues were the same then as they are now. But nineteenth century welfare was not only about deterrence. In addition to the state minimum, there was also a sense of 'community without politics' which enjoined the successful to help the less fortunate and the less fortunate to fight their way to independence, if it was at all possible.

Field understands that there was this tradition of 'social collectivism' but confuses it with national insurance based on 'stakeholder' control rather than political direction. Stakeholder control of a national insurance corporation, however, is not the same as community without politics. It remains an essentially political system. In Oakeshott's language, Field is nearer to the model of corporate association than to the ethos of civil association.

There is also a more pragmatic argument for permitting the variety that would be suppressed by compulsory insurance. The labour market has become more flexible in recent years and there is more job insecurity, but the implication of this change is that *less* compulsion would be better for individual workers. Without compulsory national insurance, people will be more free to provide in a multitude of ways against loss of earnings due to unemployment or ill health (perhaps along the historical lines described earlier, p. 147). Competition and variety of provision will create far more flexibility than a semi-politicised public corporation which could never allow room for the many different circumstances in which people find themselves. Less compulsion will permit more customised solutions to emerge.

To sum up: my main criticism of Field's scheme is that he mistakenly believes that a national insurance system can strengthen character when it has historically had the reverse effect. What is missing from his scheme is mutual respect. The tradition of strict poor law administration did not exist in isolation and was only morally defensible because it was associated with the ethos of community without politics. Its aim was independence, not for its own sake, but to allow people to put something back. Responsibility has a wider meaning than 'blame'. And stigma is not a permanent condition, but a stimulus to be a better person. The same is true today. Tightening up the social security system should be accompanied by the rebuilding of the whole three-part ethos of the past—a state minimum; personal (or mutual) responsibility; and community without politics. Compulsory national insurance will obstruct its re-emergence, not assist it.

Conclusion

The ruling principle of the present system is universalism at the expense of all else. The alternative system proposed here would allow the exercise of free scope by individuals to provide in a variety of ways against contingencies. It would be based on a safety net designed to restore independence and encourage assistance based on mutual respect, not 'resource rights'. And it would foster renewed strength of character through the exercise of responsibility.

Field's criticism is of seminal importance because it seeks to re-moralise welfare policy. But the radicalism of his analysis is not carried through into the design of his proposals.

Contrary to the caricature fostered by some social-policy analysts, private help does not imply one-sided gratitude, but mutual respect. Political help, however, implies political gratitude. Politicians who promise to provide for all our cares at the expense of other taxpayers appeal to human weaknesses. Such politicians seek to manipulate those who are unsure of their ability to cope with modern pressures by encouraging their lack of independence instead of seeking to bring out the best in them. Civil association rests on the view that we grow by facing challenges, and improve by bearing responsibility for overcoming the difficulties we face. The present welfare mentality assumes a system of leaders and followers, but while the political leaders may claim to serve their followers, they do not respect them.

Notes

Preface

1 For an excellent discussion of the post-communist mood see Skidelsky, R., *The World After Communism*, London: Macmillan, 1995.

Chapter 1

1 *The Observer*, 14 May 1995.

2 Many such studies were published by the Institute of Economic Affairs in the 1960s and 1970s when it was under the leadership of Ralph Harris and Arthur Seldon.

3 Shirley Letwin, *The Anatomy of Thatcherism*, London: Fontana, 1992, pp. 32-36.

Chapter 2

1 Hayek, F.A., *The Intellectuals and Socialism*, Fairfax: Institute for Humane Studies, 1990, (first published 1949) pp. 26-27.

2 Oakeshott, M., *On Human Conduct*, Oxford: Clarendon Press, 1975, p. 222.

3 *Ibid.*, pp. 313-14.

4 *Ibid.*, p. 318.

5 *Ibid.*, p. 276; p. 237.

6 Michael Novak makes a similar point by distinguishing between the 'person' and the 'individual', in *Free Persons and the Common Good*, London: Madison Books, 1989, pp. 32-33.

7 Hayek, F.A., *Individualism and Economic Order*, London: Routledge & Kegan Paul 1949, p. 6.

8 For example, Norman Barry, *On Classical Liberalism and Libertarianism*, London: Macmillan, 1986.

9 In Acton, *Essays in the History of Liberty*. Indianapolis: Liberty Fund, 1986, p. 200.

10 Gray, J., *The Undoing of Conservatism*, London: Social Market Foundation, 1994, p. 11.

11 *The Undoing of Conservatism*, pp. 26-27.

12 Smith, A., *The Theory of Moral Sentiments*, Indianapolis: Liberty Fund, 1976, p. 48.

13 *Ibid.*, p. 212. (Emphasis added.)

14 *Ibid.*, p. 227.

15 Smith, *The Theory of Moral Sentiments*, p. 72; see also West, E.G., *Adam Smith: The Man and his Works*, Indianapolis: Liberty Press, 1976.

16 Lord Acton, 'Freedom in Antiquity', in *The History of Freedom and Other Essays*, London: Macmillan, 1907, p. 3.

17 *The Theory of Moral Sentiments*, pp. 228-29.

18 Stewart, Dugald, 'Account of the life and writings of Adam Smith' in Smith, A., *Essays on Philosophical Subjects*, Indianapolis: Liberty Fund, 1982; Jerry Z. Muller, *Adam Smith in His Time and Ours*, New York: The Free Press, 1993; West, E.G., *Adam Smith: The Man and his Works*, Indianapolis: Liberty Press, 1976.

19 Aristotle, 'The Nicomachean Ethics' in *The Ethics of Aristotle*, Harmondsworth: Penguin, 1976, pp. 91-92; p. 95.

20 Smith, A., *Lectures on Jurisprudence*, Indianapolis: Liberty Fund, 1982, pp. 142-43.

21 Smith, *The Theory of Moral Sentiments*, p. 364.

22 Wilson, J.Q., *The Moral Sense*, New York: Free Press, 1993, p. 249.

23 *Ibid.*, pp. 162-63.

24 *The Theory of Moral Sentiments*, pp. 283-84.

25 *Ibid.*, p. 269.

26 *Ibid.*, pp. 71-72.

27 Quoted in Novak, M., *The Catholic Ethic and the Spirit of Capitalism*, New York: Free Press, 1993, pp. 316-17, note 4.

28 Röpke, W., *A Humane Economy*, London: Oswald Wolff, 1960, p. 123; p. 116.

29 *Ibid.*, p. 117-18; pp. 121-23.

30 *Ibid.*, p. 124.

31 *Ibid.*, p. 125.

32 Knight, F., *Freedom and Reform*, Indianapolis: Liberty Press, 1982, p. 477.

33 Röpke, *A Humane Economy*, p. 138.

34 Tocqueville, Alexis de, *Democracy in America*, New York: Vintage Books, 1990, vol. 2, p. 127.

35 Rousseau, E., 'A Discourse on the Origin of Inequality', in *The Social Contract and Discourses*, London: Dent, 1973, p. 68.

36 Hayek, *F.A., The Fatal Conceit*, London: Routledge, 1988, Chapter 9.

37 *Ibid.*, pp. 21-23.

38 William Blackstone, *Commentaries on the Laws of England*, (Facsimile of First Edition of 1765-1769) vol. 1, Chicago: University of Chicago Press, 1979, pp. 38-62.

39 Smith, A., *An Inquiry Into the Nature and Causes of the Wealth of Nations,* Indianapolis: Liberty Press, 1976, vol. 2, p. 910.

40 Smith, *Wealth of Nations,* p. 610.

41 Brittan, S., *A Restatement of Economic Liberalism,* London: Macmillan, 1988, p. 310; p. 243.

42 *A Restatement of Economic Liberalism,* p. 315; see also Brittan, S., *Capitalism With a Human Face,* London: Edward Elgar, 1995, p. 282.

43 Bennett, W.J., *The Book of Virtues,* New York: Simon and Schuster, 1993.

44 *Theory of Moral Sentiments,* p. 392.

45 Buchanan, J.M. *What Should Economists Do?,* Indianapolis: Liberty Fund, 1979, p. 217; pp. 208-09.

46 Hayek, *The Fatal Conceit,* p. 136.

47 *Ibid.,* p. 137.

48 Hayek, F. A., 'Opening address to a conference at Mont Pelerin', in *Studies in Philosophy, Politics and Economics*. London: Routledge & Kegan Paul, 1967, p. 155.

49 Magnet, M., *The Dream and the Nightmare,* New York: William Morrow, 1993, p. 17.

50 Magnet, *The Dream and the Nightmare,* p. 18.

51 Magnet's analysis is supported by Norman Dennis' discussions of British cultural change in *Families Without Fatherhood* (co-authored with George Erdos; 2nd edn., London: IEA, 1993) and *Rising Crime and the Dismembered Family,* London: IEA, 1993.

52 Magnet, *The Dream and the Nightmare,* p. 19.

53 Smith, *Wealth of Nations,* p. 794.

54 Hayek, *The Constitution of Liberty,* p. 17.

55 *Ibid.,* p. 16.

56 Oakeshott, M., 'The Tower of Babel' in *Rationalism in Politics and Other Essays,* Indianapolis: Liberty Press, 1991, p. 482.

57 Oakeshott, 'The Tower of Babel', p. 466.

58 *Ibid.,* p. 471.

59 *Ibid.,* p. 472.

60 Becker, Gary S., *The Economic Approach to Human Behaviour*. Chicago: University of Chicago Press, 1976, p. 8; p. 14.

61 *Ibid.,* p. 10.

62 Tullock, G., *The Vote Motive,* London: Institute of Economic Affairs, 1976, pp. 26-7.

63 *Ibid.,* p. 28.

64 *Ibid.,* pp. 29-30.

65 Knight, F. 'Ethics and Economic Reform', in *Freedom and Reform*, Indianapolis: Liberty Press, 1982, pp. 63-64.

66 Buchanan, J., 'Foreword' in Knight, F.H., *Freedom and Reform*, p. xii.

67 Buchanan, *What Should Economists Do?*, p. 98.

68 *Ibid.*, p. 112.

69 *Ibid.*, p. 94.

70 *Ibid.*, p. 102.

71 Röpke, *A Humane Economy*, pp. 90-91; p. 93.

72 *Ibid.*, p. 94.

73 *Ibid.*, p. 101.

74 *Ibid.*, p. 107.

75 *Ibid.*, p. 109.

76 *Ibid.*, p. 110.

77 As de Jasay demonstrated: de Jasay, A., *Market Socialism: A Scrutiny*, London: IEA, 1990.

78 Hayek, *The Fatal Conceit*, pp. 21-22.

Chapter 3

1 Oakeshott, M., *On Human Conduct*, Oxford: Clarendon Press, 1975, p. 220.

2 Smith, A., *Wealth of Nations*, Indianapolis: Liberty Fund, 1981, pp. 802-3.

3 Oakeshott, *On Human Conduct*, p. 222.

4 *Ibid.*, p. 284.

5 *Ibid.*, pp. 288, 290.

6 *Ibid.*, pp. 291, 293.

7 *Fabian Essays*, p. 54, in Oakeshott, *On Human Conduct*, p. 300.

8 Brittan, S., *A Restatement of Economic Liberalism*, London: Macmillan, 1988, pp. 107-8.

9 Hayek, F.A., *Law, Legislation and Liberty*, London: Routledge & Kegan Paul, 1973, vol. 1, p. 2.

10 Oakeshott, *On Human Conduct*, p. 318.

11 Harris, R. and Seldon, A., *Over-Ruled on Welfare*, London: IEA, 1979.

12 Olson, M., *The Logic of Collective Action*, Cambridge, Mass: Harvard University Press, 1971; *The Rise and Decline of Nations*, New Haven: Yale University Press, 1982.

13 Seldon, A., *Capitalism*, Oxford: Blackwell, 1990, p. 6.

14 Friedman, M. and R., *Free to Choose,* London: Secker and Warburg, 1980, p. 107.

15 Le Grand, J., *The Strategy of Equality,* London: George Allen & Unwin, 1982, pp. 4-5.

16 Thomson, D., *Selfish Generations?,* Wellington: Bridget Williams, 1991.

17 Will Hutton, *The State We're In,* London: Jonathan Cape, 1995, pp. 286-88.

18 Oakeshott, *On Human Conduct,* p. 309; p. 308.

19 *Ibid.,* p. 307.

20 *Ibid.,* p. 275.

21 *Ibid.,* p. 278.

22 Quoted in Charles Sykes, *A Nation of Victims, The Decay of American Character,* New York: St Martin's Press, 1992, p. 13.

23 Sykes, *A Nation of Victims,* p. 69.

24 Niebuhr quoted in Sykes, *A Nation of Victims,* p. 70.

25 Quoted in Sykes, *A Nation of Victims,* pp. 70-71.

26 Quoted in Sykes, *A Nation of Victims,* p. 71.

27 *Ibid.,* p. 69; p. 73.

28 Quoted in Sykes, *A Nation of Victims,* p. 84.

29 Quoted in Sykes, *A Nation of Victims,* p. 105.

30 Ryan, William, *Blaming the Victim,* 2nd Edn, New York: Vintage Books, 1976.

31 Ryan, *Blaming the Victim,* p. 44; p. 52.

32 *Ibid.,* p. 53.

33 *Ibid.,* pp. 114-15.

34 *Ibid.,* p. 72.

35 *Ibid.,* pp. 196-97; p. 212.

36 *Ibid.,* pp. 284-85.

37 Sykes, *A Nation of Victims,* p. 144.

38 *Ibid.,* p. 18; p. 11.

39 *Ibid.,* p. 7; p. 17; p. 168.

40 *Ibid.,* p. 16.

41 This section updates some parts of the now out-of-print *Equalising People* (London: IEA, 1990).

42 Rowntree, B.S., *Poverty: A Study of Town Life,* 2nd Edn., London: Thomas Nelson, reprint, approx. 1901, p. 117.

43 *Joseph Rowntree Foundation Inquiry into Income and Wealth,* York: Joseph Rowntree Foundation, 1995, vol. 1, p. 6.

44 *Ibid.*, vol. 1, p. 6.

45 *Ibid.*, vol. 1, p. 15.

46 Joseph Rowntree Foundation, Press Release, 9 February 1995, p. 4.

47 See for example, Walker, A. and Walker, C. (eds.), *The Growing Divide: A Social Audit 1979-1987*, London: Child Poverty Action Group, 1987.

48 Oppenheim, C., *Poverty: the Facts*, London: CPAG, 1993, pp. 39-53.

49 Circular letter to CPAG members, 21 June 1995, from Sally Witcher, Director.

50 Peter Golding in Middleton, S., Ashworth, K. and Walker, R., *Family Fortunes*, London: CPAG, 1994, p. ix.

51 *The New Review (Low Pay Unit)*, Jan/Feb 1995, p. 5; p. 10.

52 Goodman, A. and Webb, S., *The Distribution of UK Household Expenditure 1979-1992*, London: Institute for Fiscal Studies, 1995, p. 11.

53 *Ibid.*, p. 15.

54 *Ibid.*, p. 25.

55 *Ibid.*, p. 29.

56 *Ibid.*, p. 27, Figure 5.3.

57 *Ibid.*, p. 30.

58 *Ibid.*, p. 29.

59 *Ibid.*, pp. 30-31.

60 *Ibid.*, p. 27.

61 *Ibid.*, p. 27.

62 The IFS assessed whether this finding was the result of increased debt and found that it was not. Goodman and Webb, p. 30.

63 Department of Social Security, *Households Below Average Income, 1979-1992/93*, London: HMSO, 1995, Table 9.1, p. 145.

64 Hayek, F.A., *Law, Legislation and Liberty*, London: Routledge & Kegan Paul, 1976, vol. 2, p. 74.

65 Hayek, F.A., *The Constitution of Liberty*, London: Routledge & Kegan Paul, 1960, p. 19; p. 18.

66 For a discussion of hyper-individualism see Berger, B. and Berger, P.L., *The War Over the Family*, London: Hutchinson, 1983.

67 Brittan, S., 'The Wenceslas Myth', pp. 3-4 in *The Role and Limits of Government: Essays in Political Economy*, London: Temple Smith, 1983, pp. 1-21.

68 Marshall, T.H., 'Citizenship and Social Class', in Marshall, T.H., *Sociology at the Crossroads and Other Essays*, London: Heinemann, 1963, p. 74.

69 Harris, D., *Justifying State Welfare: The New Right versus the Old Left*, Oxford: Blackwell, 1987, p. 148.

70 Thomson, D., *Selfish Generations?*, Wellington: Bridget Williams, 1991; Le Grand, J. and Goodin, R.E., *The Middle Class Infiltration of the Welfare state: Some Evidence From Australia*, London School of Economics, Welfare State Programme, Discussion Paper 10, 1986; Le Grand, J. and Winter, D., *The Middle Classes and the Welfare State*, London School of Economics, Welfare State Programme, Discussion Paper 14, 1987.

71 Quoted in Harris, D., *Justifying State Welfare*, p. 59.

72 Harris, *Justifying State Welfare*, pp. 78-79.

73 de Jouvenel, B., *The Ethics of Redistribution*, p. 53.

74 Quoted in Himmelfarb, G., *Poverty and Compassion*, New York: Knopf, 1991, p. 205.

75 *Ibid.*, p. 205.

76 *Ibid.*, pp. 236-37.

77 *Ibid.*, p. 198.

78 Webb, B., *My Apprenticeship*. London: Longmans, 1926, p. 143.

79 De Jouvenel, B., *The Ethics of Redistribution*, Cambridge: Cambridge University Press, 1951, p. 12.

80 *Ibid.*, p. 48.

81 Rawls, J., *A Theory of Justice*, Oxford: Oxford University Press, 1973, p. 12.

82 *Ibid.*, p. 302; pp. 284-93; p. 303.

83 Nozick, R., *Anarchy, State and Utopia*, Oxford: Blackwell, 1974, p. 190; pp. 201-02; pp. 186-87.

84 Rawls, *A Theory of Justice*.

85 Hayek, F.A., *Law, Legislation and Liberty*, vol. 2, p. 130.

86 *Ibid.*, vol. 2, p. 132.

87 Green, D.G., *Equalizing People*, London: IEA, 1990.

Chapter 4

1 Friedman, M. and Friedman, R., *Free to Choose*, 1980, p. 119.

2 *Ibid.*, p. 120.

3 Anderson, M., *Welfare*, Stanford: Hoover Institution, 1978.

4 Wilson, J.Q. and Herrnstein, R., *Crime and Human Nature*, New York: Simon & Schuster, 1985, p. 431.

5 *Ibid.*, p. 528.

6 Wilson, J.Q., *On Character*, Washington, DC: AEI, 1991, p. 17.

7 Murray, C., *Losing Ground: American Social Policy, 1950-1980*, New York: Basic Books, 1984, p. 25.

8 Murray, C., 'Welfare and the Family: the US Experience', *Journal of Labour Economics*, 1993, vol. 11, no. 1, pat. 2, p. 232.

9 Murray, *Losing Ground*, p. 14.

10 *Ibid.*, p. 48.

11 *Ibid.*, p. 8.

12 *Ibid.*, p. 76.

13 *Ibid.*, p. 126; p. 130.

14 Mead, L., *Beyond Entitlement: The Social Obligations of Citizenship*, New York: The Free Press, 1986, p. 64.

15 Murray, *Losing Ground*, pp. 151-52.

16 *Ibid.*, p. 179.

17 Mead, *Beyond Entitlement*, p. 21; p. 68.

18 *Ibid.*, p. 24.

19 *Ibid.*, p. 57.

20 *Ibid.*, p. 59.

21 *Ibid.*, p. 179.

22 *Ibid.*, p. 178.

23 *Ibid.*, p. 46.

24 *Ibid.*, p. 49.

25 *Ibid.*, pp. 255-56.

26 *Ibid.*, pp. 242-43.

27 *Ibid.*, p. 110.

28 *Ibid.*, p. 82.

29 *Ibid.*, p. 89; p. 90.

30 Mead, L., *The New Politics of Poverty*, New York: Basic Books, 1992, p. x.

31 Magnet, *The Dream and the Nightmare*, 1993, p. 16.

32 *Ibid.*, p. 16.

33 *Ibid.*, p. 17.

34 Murray, *Losing Ground*, p. 179.

35 Magnet, *The Dream and the Nightmare*, pp. 33-34.

36 *Ibid.*, p. 46.

37 *Ibid.*, p. 21.

38 Murray, C., *The Emerging British Underclass*, London: IEA, 1990.

39 Murray, C., *Underclass: The Crisis Deepens*, London: IEA, 1994.

40 *Social Trends*, London: HMSO, 1995, p. 43.

41 *Ibid.*, p. 41.

42 *Ibid.*, p. 43.

43 Murray, *Wall Street Journal Europe*, 16 November 1993.

44 *Birth Statistics*, London: HMSO, 1992, p. xxvi, pp. 15-17.

45 Kiernan, K.E., *Transition to Parenthood: Young Mothers, Young Fathers—Associated Factors and Later Life Experiences*, Welfare State Programme, London School of Economics, Discussion Paper WSP/113, July 1995, pp. 37-38.

46 *Social Trends*, London: HMSO, 1994, p. 38.

47 *Marriage and Divorce Statistics*, London: HMSO, 1993, Series FM2, no, 21, p. 64; *Social Trends*, 1995, p. 36.

48 *Marriage and Divorce Statistics*, 1993, Series FM2, no, 21, p. 65.

49 *Social Trends*, 1995, p. 34.

50 Haskey, J., 'Trends in the Numbers of One-parent Families in Great Britain', *Population Trends*, No. 71, Spring 1993, London: HMSO, pp. 26-33; Haskey, J., 'Estimated Numbers of One-parent Families and Their Prevalence in Great Britain in 1991', *Population Trends*, no. 78, Winter 1994, p. 6.

51 Haskey, J., 'Estimated Numbers of One-parent Families and Their Prevalence in Great Britain in 1991', *Population Trends*, no. 78, Winter 1994, London: HMSO, p. 7.

52 Department of Social Security, *Social Security Statistics 1994*, London: HMSO, 1994, p. 26.

53 Morgan, P., *Farewell to the Family*, London: IEA, 1995.

54 Murray, *Underclass: The Crisis Deepens*, p. 23.

55 *Underclass: The Crisis Deepens*, pp. 24-25.

56 Crellin, E., Kellmer Pringle M.L., and West, P., *Born Illegitimate: Social and Economic Implications*, Windsor, England: NFER, 1971, p. 53. (Quoted in Dennis, N. and Erdos, G., *Families Without Fatherhood*, 2nd edn., London: IEA, 1993.)

57 *Born Illegitimate*, p. 55; p. 68.

58 *Ibid.*, p. 68.

59 *Ibid.*, p. 74.

60 *Ibid.*, p. 160.

61 *Ibid.*, p. 83; p. 161.

62 Barbara Dafoe Whitehead, 'Dan Quayle Was Right', *The Atlantic Monthly*, April 1993, p. 47. The article provides a valuable summary of the American evidence.

63 'Family Structure and Children's Health: United States, 1988', *Vital and Health Statistics,* series 10, no. 178, June 1991. On a very few measures the children of lone parents in the highest income group (over $50,000) did well but, according to a private conversation with Deborah A. Dawson, the chief researcher, these finding for the highest income group were due to the small size of this group in the total sample. For example, there may well have been no lone parents earning $50,000 whose children suffered from problems such as bed-wetting.

64 Murray, *Losing Ground*, p. 114.

65 *Ibid.*, p. 115.

66 Dennis, N., *Rising Crime and the Dismembered Family*, London: IEA, 1993, p. 1.

67 *Ibid.*, pp. 1-2.

68 *Ibid.*, p. 2.

69 The rates are 'notifiable offences reported to the police, excluding other criminal damage valued at £20 or under, per 100,000 population per annum'. Home Office, *Criminal Statistics England and Wales 1991*, Cm 2134, London: HMSO, February 1993.

70 Murray, *Underclass: The Crisis Deepens*, p. 2.

71 Dennis, N. and Halsey, A.H., *English Ethical Socialism*, Oxford: Clarendon Press, 1988.

72 Field, F., *Making Welfare Work: Reconstructing Welfare for the Millennium*, London: Institute of Community Studies, 1995, p. 1.

73 *Ibid.*, p. 10 (emphasis in original).

74 *Ibid.*, pp. 80-82.

75 *Ibid.*, pp. 90-92.

76 According to the Department of Social Security, 25% of families are in receipt of at least one major means-tested benefit. These families comprise about 27% of the population. This estimate was supplied in a personal communication by the DSS Analytical Services Division; see also *Independent*, 19 August 1993.

77 *Making Welfare Work*, p. 22.

78 Selbourne, D., *The Principle of Duty*, London: Sinclair-Stevenson, 1994, p. 58; p. 59.

79 *Ibid.*, p. 60.

80 Mill, J.S., *Principles of Political Economy*, (Edited by W.J. Ashley) London: Longmans, 1909, p. 948.

81 Mill, *Principles of Political Economy*, pp. 948-49.

Chapter 5

1 Blackstone, W., *Commentaries on the Laws of England*, (4 volume facsimile of 1765 edition), Chicago: University of Chicago Press, 1979, vol. 1., p. 42.

2 *Commentaries on the Laws of England*, vol. 1., p. 53.

3 Hume, D., *The History of England*, 1778 edition, Indianapolis: Liberty Classics, 1983, vol. V, pp. 42-43.

4 *Commentaries on the Laws of England*, vol. 1., p. 44.

5 Hayek, *Law, Legislation and Liberty*, vol. 3, pp. 112-13.

6 Smiles, S., *Character*, London: John Murray, 1896, p. 3.

7 *Ibid.*, p. 4.

8 *Ibid.*, pp. 4-5.

9 Himmelfarb, G. *The De-moralisation of Society*, London: IEA, 1995, p. 15.

10 Burke, E., 'Letter to a Member of the National Assembly', *Works*, (World's Classics edn.) Oxford: Oxford University Press, 1907, vol. iv, p. 319.

11 Knight, F., 'Social Science and the Political Trend', in *Freedom and Reform*, Indianapolis: Liberty Press, 1982, pp. 32-33.

12 Smith, *The Theory of Moral Sentiments*, p. 159.

13 Smith, *Lectures on Jurisprudence*, p. 160.

14 *Ibid.*, p. 160.

15 Emphasis added.

16 Mill, *Principles of Political Economy*, pp. 967-68.

17 *Ibid.*, p. 969.

18 Himmelfarb, *The De-moralisation of Society*.

19 For a discussion of stigma see Pinker, R, *Social Theory and Social Policy*, London: Heinemann, 1971, Chapter 4.

20 Loch, C.S., *Charity and Social Life*, London: Macmillan, 1910, p. 387.

21 *Ibid.*, p. 401.

22 *Ibid.*, p. 369.

23 Himmelfarb, G., *Poverty and Compassion*, New York: Knopf, 1991, p. 204.

24 *Ibid.*, p. 190.

25 Loch, *Charity and Social Life*, p. 400.

26 Himmelfarb, *Poverty and Compassion*, p. 198.

27 Dickens, C., *Hard Times*, London: Pan Books, 1977, pp. 165-66.

28 Prochaska, F.K., *Women and Philanthropy in Nineteenth-Century England*, Oxford: Clarendon Press, 1980, pp. 113-14.

29 Collini, S., *Public Moralists*, Oxford: Clarendon Press, 1993, p. 93.

30 Marshall, A., 'Social Possibilities of economic chivalry', in Pigou, A.C. (ed) *Memorials of Alfred Marshall*, New York: Kelley & Millman, 1956; Marshall, *Principles of Economics*, 8th edn., London: Macmillan, 1920, e.g. pp. 1-2.

31 Himmelfarb, *Poverty and Compassion*, p. 199.

32 Loch, *Charity and Social Life*, p. 367.

33 *Ibid.*, pp. 367-68.

34 Finlayson, G., *Citizen, State, and Social Welfare in Britain 1830-1990*, Oxford: Clarendon Press, 1994, p. 63; Royal Commission on the Poor Laws, *Report*, London: HMSO, 1909, p. 26.

35 For a fuller discussion of British friendly societies see Green, D.G., *Reinventing Civil Society*.

36 Ancient Order of Foresters, Lecture 3, 1879.

37 *Foresters Miscellany*, January 1882, p. 6.

38 Royal Commission on the Poor Laws, Appendix VII, 1909, Qs. 77543-44.

39 Royal Commission on the Poor Laws, *Report*, 1909, para. 22.

40 Royal Commission on the Poor Laws, *Report*, Part III, 'Historical Sketch of the Poor Laws Down to 1834', pp. 55-57.

Chapter 6

1 Beveridge, W., *Voluntary Action*, London: George Allen & Unwin, 1948, p. 7.

2 Novak, M. (ed.), *The New Consensus on Family and Welfare*, Washington DC: American Enterprise Institute, 1987.

3 Quoted in *The Times*, 4 October 1995, p. 16.

4 A point emphasised by Hayek, and long-argued by Richard Cornuelle in *Reclaiming the American Dream*, New York: Vintage, 1965.

5 See Green, D.G., *Reinventing Civil Society*, London: IEA, 1993.

6 For another view see, Knight, B., *Voluntary Action*, London: Centris, 1993.

7 Green, *Reinventing Civil Society*.

8 McBriar, A.M., *An Edwardian Mixed Doubles*, Oxford: Clarendon Press, 1987, pp. 313-14, 318, 331-32.

9 Quoted in Hayek, *Law, Legislation and Liberty*, vol. I, p. 158, note 14.

10 Green, *Reinventing Civil Society*.

11 Beveridge, Lord, *Voluntary Action*, London: Allen & Unwin, 1948, p. 21.

12 For a fuller discussion see Green, *Reinventing Civil Society*.

13 *Voluntary Action*, p. 44.

14 *Ibid.*, pp. 45-50.

15 Wilkinson, J.F., *The Friendly Society Movement*, London: Longman, 1891, p. 193; Webb, S. and B., *Industrial Democracy*, London: The Authors, 1913, p. 101, note 1.

16 Department of Social Security, *The Growth of Social Security*, London: HMSO, 1993, p. 20.

17 Royal Commission on the Poor Laws, 1909, Appendix IV, Q. 47501.

18 Loch, C.S., *A Great Ideal and its Champion. (Papers and addresses by the late Sir Charles Stewart Loch.)* London: Allen & Unwin, 1923, p. 192.

19 Burton, J., *Would Workfare Work?*, University of Buckingham, Employment Research Centre, 1987, pp. 18-23.

20 Field, *Making Welfare Work: Reconstructing Welfare for the Millennium*, pp. 186-7.

21 *Making Welfare Work*, p. 188.

22 Segalman, R. and Marsland, D., *Cradle to Grave: Comparative Perspectives on the State of Welfare*, London: Macmillan/Social Affairs Unit, 1989, pp. 65-77.

23 Child Poverty Action Group, *National Welfare Benefits Handbook*, 1995-96, pp. 8-9.

24 *Ibid.*, p. 49; pp. 51-52.

25 Murray, C., 'What To Do About Welfare', *Commentary*, December 1994, pp. 26-34.

26 Polly Toynbee, *The Independent*, 22 March 1995; Mary Kenny, *The Sunday Telegraph*, 26 March 1995.

27 Field, F., *Making Welfare Work*, p. 124.

28 *Ibid.*, p. 125; p. 127.

29 *Ibid.*, p. 120.

30 *Ibid.*, p. 191.

31 *Ibid.*, p. 180; p. 190.

32 *Ibid.*, p. 122.

33 *Ibid.*, p. 148.

34 *Ibid.*, p. 150.

35 *Ibid.*, p. 134.

36 *Ibid.*, p. 138.

37 *Ibid.*, pp. 134-35.

38 *Ibid.*, p. 139.

39 *Ibid.*, p. 140.

40 *Ibid.*, p. 136.

41 *Ibid.*, p. 136.

42 *Ibid.*, p. 137.

Available for Half-Price

Liberating Women ... From Modern Feminism, Caroline Quest (Ed), Norman Barry, Mary Kenny, Patricia Morgan, Joan Kennedy Taylor, Glenn Wilson £6.95, 101pp, 1994, ISBN 0-255 36353-2

Caroline Quest argues that 'power feminism' ends up having as little relevance to most women as the 'victim feminism' it is directed against. It is, she says, 'for pre-maternal young women' and 'is of little relevance and help to the realities of life for the majority of real women'.

"It would be a mistake ... to take anything but seriously the essay "Double income, no kids: the case for a family wage" by the sociologist Patricia Morgan."

The Times

The Moral Foundations of Market Institutions, John Gray, with Chandran Kukathas, Patrick Minford and Raymond Plant, £7.95, 142pp, Feb 1992, ISBN: 0-255 36271-4

Distinguished Oxford philosopher, John Gray, examines the moral legitimacy of the market economy. While upholding the value of the market economy he insists on the importance of an 'enabling' welfare state.

"one of the most intelligent and sophisticated contributions to modern conservative philosophy."

The Times

"This powerful tract ... maps out a plausible middle ground for political debate."

Financial Times

The De-moralization of Society: From Victorian Virtues to Modern Values, Gertrude Himmelfarb, £12.50, 314pp, March 1995, ISBN: 0-255 36359-1

"Gertrude Himmelfarb is one of the world's most knowledgeable scholars of the British Victorian period." *The Sunday Telegraph*

"Gertrude Himmelfarb is one of America's most distinguished intellectual historians. This book will only enhance that reputation." William J. Bennett

Farewell to the Family? Public Policy and Family Breakdown in Britain and the USA, PATRICIA MORGAN, £9.00 175pp, Jan 1995, ISBN: 0-255 36356-7

"Tougher policies to promote family life are being demanded by Tory MPs following a report accusing the Government of discriminating against married couples in favour of lone parents."

The Daily Telegraph

ORDER FORM—EVERYTHING HALF-PRICE

Title	Normal Price	Offer Price	Qty	£
Families Without Fatherhood (2nd Edition)	£7.95	£3.95		
Rising Crime and the Dismembered Family	£5.95	£2.95		
Reinventing Civil Society	£7.95	£3.95		
A Moral Basis for Liberty	£4.95	£2.45		
The Family: Just Another Lifestyle Choice?	£6.95	£3.45		
Equal Opportunities: A Feminist Fallacy	£6.95	£3.45		
Moral Foundations of Market Institutions	£7.95	£3.95		
The Emerging British Underclass	£5.95	£2.95		
Farewell to the Family	£9.00	£4.50		
Underclass: the Crisis Deepens	£5.99	£2.95		
God and the Marketplace	£4.90	£2.45		
The De-moralisation of Society	£12.50	£6.25		
Liberating Women From Modern Feminism	£6.95	£3.45		

Subtotal: ☐

Please add 50p P&P per book up to a maximum of £4.00

P&P: ☐

Total: ☐

✓

I enclose a cheque for £..................... payable to the Institute of Economic Affairs ☐

Please debit my Mastercard/Visa/Amex/Diner's card for £.................. ☐

Number: ....

Expiry Date: ....

Name: ....

Address: ....

....

....

Please return to ***IEA Health and Welfare Unit, Institute of Economic Affairs, 2 Lord North Street, Westminster, London SW1P 3LB***